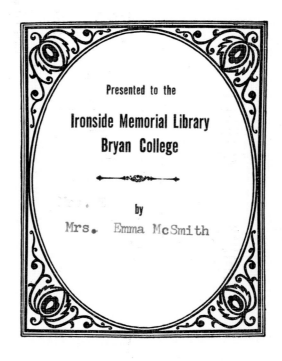

WHO IS
MY
NEIGHBOR?

Contributors

ETHEL PERCY ANDRUS

SMILEY BLANTON

JOHN S. BRADWAY

DOROTHY DAY

EBBE CURTIS HOFF

ALIDA DE JAGER

SPURGEON M. KEENY

FRANK C. LAUBACH

WALTER C. LOWDERMILK

RICHARD AMBROSE REEVES

DOUGLAS C. RIGG

HOWARD A. RUSK

MICHAEL SCOTT

GORDON S. SEAGRAVE

WHO IS MY NEIGHBOR?

Edited by ESTHER PIKE

GREENWICH · CONNECTICUT

1960

ACKNOWLEDGMENT: The Editor is grateful to the publishers and copyright holders for permission to quote the following:

Arthur Koestler, *The Sleepwalkers*.
New York: Macmillan Company, 1959.
Karl Menninger, "Verdict, Guilty—Then What?"
in *Harper's Magazine*, August 1959.

Library of Congress Catalog Card Number: 60-5373

Printed in the United States of America

Design by Lewis F. White

317-160-C-7.5

Preface

Some time ago the publishers asked me to write a book on the social application of Christianity, around the theme, Who is my neighbor? After some thought and recognition of my own limitations, I decided that those conspicuous in actually doing what the rest of us talk about could better speak to the subject—and more relevantly. Accordingly, it is my fourteen co-authors who have made this volume possible.

I want to thank each of them for his ready acceptance of my request to contribute and for the careful thought and time that went into the writing—and also for the pleasure and inspiration which was afforded me in collaborating with them. I want to thank the several friends, including the editors of Seabury Press, whom I bothered with a variety of questions and who promptly responded. I also must thank my sixteen-year-old daughter, Cathy, who came up with the Tolstoy quotation just as I was puzzling how to begin the Introduction. And if anyone senses any of my husband's thought in these pages, the suspicion is probably correct because on many occasions he readily interrupted his own work to encourage and help me.

Among the causes to which the royalties of this book are being dedicated are: World Rehabilitation Fund; United Nations Children's Fund (UNICEF); World Literacy; the International Rescue Committee, Inc.; the American Medical Center for Burma; United States Committee for Refugees; Africa Bureau in London; multi-racial work in the Diocese of Johannesburg; social relations work in the Diocese of California; The Technion for research in soil conservation; National Retired Teachers Association; American Foundation of Religion and Psychiatry; Minnesota Prisoners Aid Society; Legal Aid Committee of the North Carolina Bar Association; Committee on Society and Alcohol, Department of Social Relations, Diocese of Virginia; and *The Catholic Worker*.

There are many other important causes, of course, but these happen to be the ones with which we have been directly concerned.

ESTHER PIKE

Contents

WHICH
WAS NEIGHBOR?

THE EDITOR'S INTRODUCTION

Which Was Neighbor?

"Where could I have got it? By reason could I have arrived at knowing that I must love my neighbor and not oppress him? I was told that in my childhood, and I believed it gladly, for they told me what was already in my soul. But who discovered it? Not reason. Reason discovered the struggle for existence, and the law that requires us to oppress all who hinder the satisfaction of our desires. That is the deduction of reason. But loving one's neighbor reason could never discover, because it's irrational."

So OBSERVES Tolstoy in the words of Levin in *Anna Karenina*. In saying that love of neighbor is irrational he does not mean that it is against reason or that it is wrong. He simply means that man could not have arrived at neighborliness through reason but rather that it is a corollary of religious faith. All of this raises the old familiar questions: Who is my neighbor? Why should I care about him? Is love or duty involved? Is there any demand upon us? Does belief in God have any impact on the question or the result?

3

For some the answer is very simple: my neighbor is someone whose company I enjoy; someone who is in the same club, of the same class of society, the same race—or ethnic group—or religion. My neighbor is someone who shares my likes and dislikes, who has the same size bank account as mine, who has the same educational background that I do.

For others the answer is just a little less simple: I will choose my own associates according to my own standards, but I will help the needy here and there; I will give money; I will serve on boards of various organizations; I will participate in committees to help this or that minority group— especially if the committee consists of my own kind. And a great deal of useful work is achieved by such people regardless of motive or degree of personal involvement. We must all recognize that a gift of five dollars to the Community Chest or a fund for world relief or whatnot, given with purity of heart and sacrificial love, will not accomplish as much for a particular cause as a gift of $5,000, motivated by any number of impure social, economic, or even psychological reasons.

For still others the answer is even more complex.

The title of this introduction isn't a misprint; it is the way Jesus rephrased the lawyer's question: Who is my neighbor? The lawyer, doubtless a good Jew, wanted to do the right thing; but, as is the bent of his profession, he wanted to know exactly where he stood. Love his neighbor as himself? Certainly. Every well-instructed Jew knew that injunction. But how much love and action did it require?

Jesus never answered the question in the terms in which it was asked. He told the familiar parable of the Good Samaritan and then concluded with the question: "Which was neighbor unto him that fell among the thieves?"

This means that in the abstract there are no limits to the law of love. Existentially—that is, in terms of each one of us particularly—there are limits. For each of us different opportunities to serve arise and each of us has different capacities to serve. I cannot serve everybody in the world even if I want to. What I am judged by is, Do I serve those whom I can? The priest, the Levite, and the Samaritan, each was presented with the same opportunity. Hence Jesus' question, "Which was neighbor?" in response to the lawyer's query, "Who is my neighbor?"

This parable has been known to Western civilization for almost 2000 years, and yet most people are still thinking in the lawyer's terms. They have set limits on the commandment in terms of particular categories: the people they like, people of their same tastes or supposed intellectual level. This doesn't mean that many of these same people are not willing to help persons outside of the "in group." But there's a great difference between a gift of one's money and a gift of oneself. The Good Samaritan did open his purse to pay the room rent (and with no tax deduction in his favor, either) but not until he had done all that he could do personally to save the man who had been left by the side of the road beaten up by thugs.

The positive desire to find opportunities to serve will open our eyes and hearts to "love our neighbors," not, of course, in the sense of the affectionate love we have for our families and friends but in the sense of being concerned for others and caring about what happens to them. It would seem that one of the best ways to stimulate that desire and to cultivate the necessary accompanying imagination is the example of people who are conspicuously serving beyond the limits of their own class, race, religion, or condition. There are innumerable such, and in this volume are presented the stories of only a dozen or so with the hope that many readers will be stirred to follow the closing injunction of the parable: "Go and do thou likewise."

"Likewise": not necessarily the same things or in the same way. Take the problem of refugees. One of our essayists has gone directly among the refugees and "bound up wounds, pouring in oil and wine, and set (them) on (his) own beast, and brought (them) to an inn, and took care of (them)." But suppose a busy housewife, who realizes that her "neighbors" extend far beyond the house next door and beyond her own community and nation, has become equally stirred up about the plight of the refugees; for her to take off for Hong Kong would be, figuratively speaking, to turn her five children into refugees—not to mention her poor husband. Does this mean that the refugee cannot be her neighbor or, rather, that she cannot be neighbor to the refugee? She certainly can. She can do things without which any professional work in the field would be quite limited, if indeed not ineffectual. She can sign up to take a refugee in her own home; she can make welcome refugees in her community; she can ask her husband to help a refugee get a job; she can help develop informed interest among her friends and acquaintances in church and community groups; she can assume responsibility in local or national organizations seeking through political action to "open the doors" more widely for the refugees' emigration and to encourage our Government to share more widely our surplus goods with needy peoples. Whether or not she has much money herself, she can help get hold of other peoples' for the cause; and she can bring up her own children with a burning interest in the problem—which I expect may last through their lifetimes too. It is because of thousands of people who can do this in their own communities that Alida de Jager's work counts for something. The Good Samaritan's patient might well have died anyway had there not been an inn and an innkeeper on a safer part of the road.

Not everybody who reads Bishop Reeves' chapter "The Segregated" can head for South Africa to get into the fray (in fact if it were known that that was the purpose of the trip, a visa would probably be unobtainable). But anybody can talk about it—and that's not unimportant. We need to stir people to be concerned for these so-called "traitors"; we have to make it increasingly difficult for our United Nations delegation, for supposed diplomatic and economic reasons, to be found supporting oppressive race policy in South Africa despite the human rights issue involved—especially since the position the Communist countries, the Arab countries and Israel have been taking is more "Christian" than the way the large "Christian" nations have been voting.* Bishop Reeves and his associates in the cause have been better able to carry on because of the devoted work of many in this country and throughout the world, who have never been to South Africa and probably will never get there.

Does that mean that those of us at home can do nothing about this problem directly? Segregation is all around us, in the North as well as in the South—in our churches and neighborhoods as well as in schools. The role of the home-bound citizen is too obvious to elaborate.

And this isn't all just a matter of committees. It is important to get money to South Africa for the support of the "treason trial" defendants. It is important that a lot of people be vociferously on the right side when a Negro seeks to move into their neighborhood. It is important, too, that those who have real estate to sell or rent make it available to anyone regardless of racial or ethnic origin.

* After a bad record in the past, the U.S., doubtless due in part to criticism within this country and in part to recognition of the growing strength of African and Asian nations in the world picture, has been willing, in the last 18 months, to support mild resolutions against apartheid.

Just as one can take an active part in local as well as national organizations designed to achieve a greater measure of racial equality, one can work for better housing, improved recreational facilities for teenagers, increased opportunities for, and understanding of, the handicapped, more help for the helpless in any field in any part of the world.

And this brings up the question of motivation, adverted to earlier. Here is where religion counts most. While we want the right things done and the right positions taken— and God does, the fundamental question with him is Why? Take one example: many loyal Americans and devout Jews and Christians are worried about nuclear testing because they dread a nuclear war and/or because they agree with the group of scientists who say the radioactive fallout is greater than our capacity healthily to absorb it. At the same time Communists and their fellow-travelers in this country don't want our government to continue nuclear testing. The common position of these two groups may or may not be entirely right; but the motivations differ radically.

Take another example: a government administrator—or for that matter, Senator—may be eager to send food or medical supplies to Belgravia, because he thinks it may help support a right-wing totalitarian government against a restless people who are willing to call themselves "communist" simply because they are ill and hungry. Another administrator or Senator agrees thoroughly with the plan, but puts his strength behind it principally because he wants sick people to be healed and hungry people to be fed. I use the word "principally" because one cannot, in terms of a given individual, entirely bifurcate the two motives. The humanitarian is, of course, glad that such a policy might help our country against the Communist empire; the "anti-Communist" certainly doesn't mind that people are also being helped.

Another example: right-wingers in our country generally

don't want more people to come into the country unless they are from the same places from which they or their forebears came. Yet an amazing number of these have associated themselves with movements designed to liberalize legislation for the admission of refugees from behind the Iron Curtain (though these folks are quite different than those favored by the Walter-McCarran Act), simply because these people were anti-Soviet. Others are for identically the same end because the refugees are homeless and in distress. Refugees can be treated as things or people.

Many motives—and mixtures of motives—enter in: a bored wife joins a committee because she is bored; a "social climber" agrees to work on a worthwhile community project because the others involved are "important"; a proud aunt because of family pride goes "all out" for her nephew's "pet charity"; the putative politician joins a "safe" cause because he thinks it will be good for his "record" some future November; the wealthy philanthropist is sometimes more interested in the tax aspects of philanthropic investments than in the human aspects.

In short, people can do the same things—and the same good things—for quite a variety of reasons. Mere mortals can only judge the merits of the causes themselves. God judges the motive, and knows whether it is truly religious. "Pure religion and undefiled before God and the Father is this, To visit the fatherless and widows in their affliction, and to keep himself unspotted from the world."

But people with quite different motivations will in fact find themselves associated together in the same cause. Each of us had better look to his own motivation, and of no one infer "guilt by association." The question, on the human level, is: Is the cause good? should the thing be done? Let God read the hearts; let's get on with the job. A peculiar assortment of people should find themselves

working for the same cause and not worrying too much
about everyone else who is *for* that particular cause being
stereotypes of themselves; a board doesn't have to be monochrome to accomplish the purpose for which it was set up.

People are sometimes inclined to think (and this can be a
convenient rationalization for inaction) that these particular
personal efforts accomplish nothing. The problem is too big,
they say. Actually, nothing gets done on the national or
international level apart from the pressure of public opinion
from below. And if the immediacies in one's life are too
time-consuming even for local committee work, one can still
manage enough time to read a good newspaper as well as
news magazines and journals of opinion, enabling him to
keep informed on matters of human concern, to develop
some zeal about some of them, and to talk about them.
Public opinion is often being formed by informed people
speaking their minds at social occasions.

Thus all of us, whether or not we are able to do the
dramatic things possible to the authors of these essays, can
be neighbor to those fallen among thieves—and we don't
have to be too literal about this phrase. It is only by analogy
that it applies to all of the categories here covered; and,
of course, there are many important areas of concern not included. A book can only be so thick, and even if all of the
obvious categories were covered it would be impossible to
treat systematically the total opportunity of service. Every
day each of us has a chance to bring something to someone
with whom circumstances bring us into contact. There are
needs of love and companionship, friendship and warmth,
concern and interest, entirely apart from more apparent
needs. Our "neighbors" are not restricted to the poor and
homeless. Neighbors in need can include ordinary citizens, the well-fixed, our own friends and relatives, our

employers and employees, our co-workers, etc. How many such opportunities of need we sense depends upon how open our eyes are. The priest and the Levite "looked" and "passed by." Some people don't even look. One object of these chapters is to help people see.

Very few of the essayists are preaching sermons, and not many advert to the relationship of theology and social ethics. In selecting them I haven't been particularly interested in their personal religious affiliations. Among those asked to write chapters have been Roman Catholics, Anglicans, Protestants, Jews, and humanists—and some whose convictions I don't know and about which I didn't ask. Some familiar texts are perhaps forceful here: "By their fruits ye shall know them" and "Inasmuch as ye have done it to one of the least of my brethren, ye have done it unto me" and "He that doeth the will of my Father shall know the truth."

At the time of the confluence of the Graeco-Roman civilization and the new Christian movement it would have been fairly easy to distinguish between those concerned for the unfortunate and those not. The former would be Jews and Christians; the latter would be pagans. Today we are in the midst of a Judaeo-Christian culture, the influence of which has permeated all of Western civilization. But there is a mixture of reactions to the *source* of this cultural influence— pro, con, and indifferent. Some well-intentioned people give conscious and active support to the spiritual and ethical well-spring of our culture; others, through inattention or pre-occupation with other matters, do not; some, through intellectual or emotional difficulties, are consciously against the religious presuppositions. But oddly enough, there is no simple identification between this threefold division and the degree of neighborliness displayed.

In fact some most violently against the dogma are the

most active and admirable in displaying the ethic. These might well ponder whether there is not an obligation to reinvest in the capital from which has come the interest although this might involve a change in personal meaning and ethic as well as social ethic. The injunction to "love thy neighbor as thyself" is a corollary to the great commandment to "love the Lord thy God with all thy heart, and with all thy soul, and with all thy mind." But that is another subject. The fact is that we have to grant that in considering the implications—in our time—of the Judaeo-Christian ethical demand in the social-political realm, those who are not conscious adherents of the source of this demand are sometimes better witnesses than those who can sincerely recite the Nicene Creed.

From a Christian perspective one can see the goodness of such persons as a witness to the Faith whether or not they see it as such themselves. From a secularist point of view one can see the same manifestation of goodness as evidence that ethical concern need not have any religious foundation. Neither point is provable.

One reason why some thoughtful people are not "sold" on the Church is that they haven't seen sufficient evidence of its active concern (apart from "words" and "resolutions") for these pressing problems. While the Church is actually doing more than some people realize (for example, the World Council of Churches refugee and relief programs), yet, particularly on the local level, the Church's action seems to fall far short of its words. On the matter of segregation undoubtedly the teaching of the churches and repeated resolutions of national church bodies contributed to the general change of climate of which the Supreme Court decisions are a symbol; but, once the decisions were rendered, we see the institutions of our secular society becoming more "Christian" than the Church in its own institutional life, especially on the local level. Right next door to an integrated public school we might see a totally monochrome church and perhaps, in the same community, a totally segregated church school, the "Christian" board members having resolved that it is "inexpedient" to admit a Negro. In some areas where Protestant churches are setting up parochial schools, a partial measure of the lay motivation appears to be coming from a last-ditch attempt to maintain segregated education, and not all of the clergy caught up in such situations have the courage (or authority) of the late Archbishop Rummel of New Orleans. This sort of thing does not exactly provide a persuasive apologetic for Christianity.

Therefore, those in the Church should perhaps listen to the testimony of Christians and non-Christians alike who are *doing* the things that Christians talk about, whatever the conscious motivation of the doer. Those who really believe that the Christian Faith is the best grounding for social action and concern should prove it—not just by syllogism but by demonstration. "Let your light so shine before men, that they may see your good works and glorify your Father which is in heaven."

THE
PHYSICALLY
HANDICAPPED

By HOWARD A. RUSK

Those for whom life is circumscribed
by physical handicap, the disabled
from birth or by disease or accident,
the limbless and the paralyzed, are
"neighbors" to Howard Rusk.

HOWARD A. RUSK, world leader in the rehabilitation of the physically handicapped, is professor and chairman of the Department of Physical Medicine and Rehabilitation at the New York University-Bellevue Medical Center, director of their Rehabilitation Institute, and chief of the Bellevue Hospital Physical Medicine and Rehabilitation Service. He is also associate editor of *The New York Times*.

After receiving his M.D. from the University of Pennsylvania, Dr. Rusk practiced internal medicine in St. Louis, Missouri, and served as instructor at Washington University School of Medicine and associate chief-of-staff at St. Luke's Hospital. During World War II, he originated and directed the AAF Convalescent-Rehabilitation Training program, for which he was awarded the Distinguished Service Medal. From 1950 to 1957, he served as chairman of the Health Resources Advisory Committee, ODM, and of the National Advisory Committee of Selective Service. In the past several years Dr. Rusk has been consultant in rehabilitation of the United Nations.

Recently, on behalf of the United Nations, World Veterans Federation, Internal Society for the Welfare of Cripples, and the American-Korean Foundation, Dr. Rusk has observed and studied rehabilitation services in some 20 countries. In 1954, he was elected president of the International Society for the Welfare of Cripples, and is currently president of the World Rehabilitation Fund, Inc.; he is president of the Eighth World Congress of the International Society for the Welfare of Cripples in New York in 1960.

Dr. Rusk has received numerous awards from health and scientific groups, recognition by many foreign governments, and a number of honorary degrees from American colleges and universities.

In addition to numerous contributions to professional and general periodicals, Dr. Rusk is co-author of *New Hope for the Handicapped* and *Living with a Disability;* of *Rehabilitation of the Cardiovascular Patient* and *Cardiovascular Rehabilitation;* and senior author of *Rehabilitation Medicine.*

The Physically Handicapped

I CAN'T remember when I didn't want to be a doctor. When I was a boy I scrubbed floors and ran errands at the local hospital in order to be around sick people. Surgery and the smell of ether did not hold the glamour for me that it holds for most youngsters. It was people— sick people—and their suffering, their problems, and their victories that challenged me.

As a result of studying and practicing medicine for the past thirty-five years, my neighbors have been people in pain and in difficulty.

I have been fortunate in that my career in medicine in these thirty-five years has coincided with medicine's golden era. Far more scientific advances have been made in these thirty-five years than in all previous history. Before then, the saving of human life as the traditional and cherished goal of medicine was largely a matter of saving individual patients. But in the past thirty-five years, the whole character of medicine's traditional goal has been changed.

17

The expansion of research into the etiology and therapy of communicable and infectious diseases "struck specifics." The establishment of new and effective public health measures and rich findings in the basic fields gave the life-saving functions of medicine mass proportions.

These, combined with similar advances in greater availability of medical and hospital care, improved nutrition, increased education, better housing, and all the contributing factors to our unprecedented current standard of living, mean hundreds of thousands of Americans are alive today who would have died at the turn of the century with the same medical problems. Yet many of them have not come out unscathed. They have survived only to find themselves confronted with residual disability.

Roy Campanella typifies this growing number of persons in our population. When the 1958 baseball season opened, one of baseball's greatest stars was missing. Instead of being in his familiar spot behind the plate in the new uniform of a Los Angeles Dodger, Roy Campanella lay in the Community Hospital, Glen Cove, Long Island. On January 28th Campanella had been taken to this hospital when he was injured as a result of his automobile overturning on a slippery road. This year, fortunately, Roy Campanella will be back in baseball, not as a player for he still remains paralyzed, but as a special coach for the Los Angeles Dodgers.

Roy Campanella's neurological status remains about the same, but his functional progress has been tremendous. He can feed himself, assist in his dressing, type a little, and even write surprisingly well. He whizzes around his Glen Cove home in an electric wheelchair—backing, turning, going beween obstacles, traveling anywhere he wants to go. He has a specially modified chair for outdoor use in which he does his coaching.

It is ironic that many of mankind's great advances develop

out of mankind's great catastrophes. Rehabilitation of persons like Roy Campanella is an example. Prior to World War II, the use of the terms "paraplegia" and "quadriplegia" were limited almost entirely to the medical profession. They were words almost totally unfamiliar to the public. In those days when an individual like Roy Campenella "broke his neck" in an automobile accident or diving mishap, it almost always meant certain death. Then such an injury was almost synonymous with death for, due to infection, the span of life was short. Among the 400 cases of paraplegia among military personel of the United States in World War I, more than 90 per cent died in the first year.

Fortunately these infections are now largely controlled with antibiotics. Increased knowledge of biochemistry and the deconditioning phenomena of bed rest have shown that such serious complications as decubitus ulcers (bed sores), kidney infections, and decalcification of the bones can be avoided. This is done by getting patients into the standing position for an hour or two each day. Special, easily operated tilt-tables have been developed for this purpose.

In World War II there were 2,500 cases of paraplegia among the military personnel of the United States. With modern medical and surgical management these men did not die. While left with severe disabilities, their minds were alert and their hands retained good function. Most faced life with a strong desire to live it as fully as possible.

What has happened to those men is shown in a study of the Veterans Administration published in 1957. The study itself did not attempt to ascertain what percentage of our total veteran paraplegic population is employed. Its purpose was to secure detailed information on the jobs held by paraplegics so that this information could be used in vocational counseling of other paraplegics.

Among the 480 jobs of 466 paraplegic veterans were a

number that were somewhat unusual. One paralyzed veteran owns the only hospital in his town. He is not only the hospital's administrator, but also its chief surgeon, performing operations from his wheelchair. Another paralyzed veteran is a playground director, organizing recreational activities for several hundred youngsters. Still another is a minister who preaches his sermons from the wheelchair and makes his pastoral calls in his hand-controlled automobile.

The most striking fact revealed by the study, however, is not unusual occupations. It is rather the fact that these paralyzed veterans are successfully performing in all sorts of jobs. Of the group, 224 are engaged in professional, technical and managerial work, 102 in clerical and sales work, 103 in mechanical work, 34 in manual work, and 17 in farming. It shows that despite severe disability there are few vocational avenues closed to paraplegics.

Because the disability of quadriplegia is even more than that of paraplegia, the rehabilitation of the quadriplegic is much more difficult and the potentials of most quadriplegic patients more limited. Heavy reliance must be placed on "self-help" devices that have been developed to promote self-sufficiency in the rehabilitation of the quadriplegic. For the past nine years, the New York University-Bellevue Medical Center, with the aid of a March of Dimes grant from the National Foundation for Infantile Paralysis, has operated a testing and information center on such devices. Devices developed in other centers are sent to New York for evaluation and testing, and the results are then distributed throughout the world. Among such devices are those to assist such patients in eating, personal hygiene, writing, typing and use of the telephone.

The National Foundation has been a leader in the development of "self-help" devices, for quadriplegia is a frequent result of paralytic poliomyelitis. In an analysis of 64,146 cases of paralytic polio, 17.4 per cent were found to have severe paralysis of at least both arms and legs. Other leading causes of quadriplegia are diving, surf and automobile accidents, and other neurological disorders.

One of the most promising recent developments of these self-help devices is a new "mechanical muscle" demonstrated in early 1958 at a conference on human disability held under the auspices of the New York Academy of Science. The mechanical muscle, which is still highly experimental, is actually a brace plus a special plastic material that contracts live muscle, powered by carbon-dioxide gas. It was developed by Dr. Joseph Laws McKibben, an atomic physicist at Los Alamos, whose daughter is a patient at the Rancho Los Amigos Respiratory Center in Los Angeles. The daughter, now 14, was paralyzed from the neck down by polio in 1952.

As a result of modern medical management and these self-help devices, there are numerous examples of determined quadriplegics who lead busy and productive lives.

One of the leading cotton brokers of the South became a quadriplegic eight years ago as a result of an automobile accident. In addition to operating a complex and highly successful business, twelve hours a day, he participates in many other activities including deer hunting. Each year he bags his quota.

In New York City, a physician broke her neck in a fall five years ago. This resulted in complete paralysis from the upper chest down and partial paralysis of the arms. This physician, however, drives her own car, leads a busy social life, and continues active practice of psychiatry.

A lawyer almost totally paralyzed in both arms and legs for the last eleven years conducts an active law practice from his apartment on New York's East Side. Each year he travels in his wheelchair on extended business trips, and since becoming paralyzed was admitted to practice before the Supreme Court of the United States.

One of the leading executives of Pan American World Airways has worked from a wheelchair since both arms and legs were paralyzed from poliomyelitis nine years ago. Since then he has assumed additional executive responsibilities that require traveling all over the world.

One of the faculty members at Rollins College, Winter Park, Florida, transferred there eight years ago as a quadriplegic student after breaking his neck in the first play of the first game of the football season. Up until then he had been considered as a football player more than as a scholar, but at Rollins College he earned election to Phi Beta Kappa and now operates the college radio station.

When Roy Campanella was a patient at the Institute of Physical Medicine and Rehabilitation, New York University-Bellevue Medical Center, he had one painting in his room. It was a Vermont winter scene, which hung on the wall at the foot of his bed. It wasn't just another painting to the former Brooklyn catcher, for it was painted by a young artist who is also a quadriplegic like himself—paralyzed in all four extremities.

The story goes back 12 years when Gilbert Provencher, who lived in a small town near Manchester, New Hampshire, dived into a shallow pool and broke his neck. He was only 14 years of age at that time. All of the normal aspirations of any boy this age were gone in a matter of seconds—athletics, education along with his age group, and a job. Gilbert Provencher had had it. He was lucky to be alive, the lesion was so high. But sometimes he wondered if he was lucky, for he spent the next four years in a local hospital and in the family home, a tiny overcrowded house where, during the winter months, he could never go down from the second floor and outdoors.

During this agonizing period Gilbert Provencher had one burning desire—he wanted to paint. He had never painted before and wondered whether he could ever do it with his paralyzed hands. In 1951 a group of Manchester's citizens, spurred on by the appeals of a local radio sports announcer, raised funds and sent Gilbert to New York for rehabilitation training. Almost the first thing he said when he arrived was that the one thing he hoped and dreamed was that he would be able to paint.

There is one rule in rehabilitation that is unbreakable—under no circumstances should a patient ever be told what he can't do until he has been given an opportunity to try. An occupational therapist designed a special double-strap apparatus with a brush attachment that went around his left elbow. Gilbert was propped up on a tilt board to which he was strapped like a papoose. A brush was inserted in the holder. His first efforts were remarkably good. Everyone who saw them said, "I wish I could do that with two good hands."

Gilbert was given training in the activities of daily living, special devices were fitted to his paralyzed hands, and he was placed upright on the tilt board four hours daily. This was done, for by standing upright for a period of hours, the calcium does not seep out of the bones and leave them fragile, nutritional deficiencies are decreased, and urinary difficulties are much more easily overcome. Gilbert's old wheelchair was replaced by a modern one specially designed and prescribed to meet his specific needs.

Even though he spent five hours a day working on a physical program, he continued to paint. Better devices were made that gave him greater range and flexibility to reach various areas of the canvas. At first he could only paint

on one-quarter of the canvas then it had to be adjusted. This
meant that he had to paint half of his picture, looking at it
upside down.

His fellow patients gave him much encouragement and
visitors at the center were deeply impressed by his courage,
perseverance, and ability. A group of art lovers asked several
critics to look at his work. They all felt he had potential. One
said, "He has some of the qualities of Grandma Moses."

A small, informal showing of his work was arranged in
1952. Ten of his paintings were sold and he received several
commissions. He sold these for enough to allow his family,
which was in very modest circumstances, to buy a second-
hand trailer for its car and to move from the long winters of
New Hampshire to the sunshine of Florida.

A group of nationally known artists offered him a two-
year correspondence course—the Famous Artists School of
Westport, Connecticut. When he went home, he studied and
worked fourteen hours a day in water-color, pen and ink,
charcoal, and oil.

Since Gilbert and his family moved to Opa-Locka, he has
been a busy man. He helps support his family, has completed his second course with Famous Artists and has
worked on several commissions. One hangs in the lobby of
the administration building of Bay Path Junior College.
Another is a portrait of Bernard M. Baruch on his eighty-
fifth birthday.

In March, 1958, Gilbert Provencher had a one-man show
in Palm Beach sponsored by a committee of patronesses of
both art and rehabilitation, headed by Mrs. Bernard F.
Gimbel. Roy Campanella was invited, but he could not make
the short trip from the Vero Beach to Palm Beach as that
was the day he reported for work as a special coach to the
Los Angeles Dodgers' spring training camp. In a telegram to
Mrs. Gimbel, he said: "Although I have not met Gilbert

Provencher, I heard a great deal about him. His story and his paintings, one of which hung in my room, were a great source of inspiration to me in my own rehabilitation."

Paraplegia and quadriplegia are still severe disabilities, but experience shows that paraplegics and quadriplegics can live among us as our neighbors and live useful, productive, satisfying lives if they receive adequate rehabilitation services. As with any severe medical problem, providing such a service costs money, but the costs are only a fraction of the costs that would accrue if such patients remained idle and dependent upon public and family assistance.

The day-to-day experience of all practicing physicians shows that not only has there been a substantial increase in the gross number of disabled persons, but that a growing percentage of our population suffer from long-term illnesses and substantial physical impairments.

Two thousand years ago the average length of life was but twenty-five years; at the turn of the century, it was forty-nine; by 1950 it had reached sixty-seven, and we now have reached hold of the legendary three-score and ten. As a result of the lengthening of the life span, today in America more than 28,000,000 of our fellow citizens are suffering from chronic disability. Staggering as this is, we can expect it to increase in the future, for, as our population continues to grow older, the incidence of chronic disability and its resultant physical disability will continue to increase correspondingly.

Using the longevity scale of various animals, some biologists have predicted that theoretically all men could live to be about 110 if the hostile forces of environment were eliminated. Dr. Louis I. Dublin, known as the dean of American health statistics, has reported recently that this does not prove out in actuality even though it may be true theoretically. He agrees that Americans will continue to make great

strides in health in the remaining forty-two years of this
century, but he says they will not gain nearly as many years
of life as they did between 1900 and 1958.

Future savings in mortality must come largely from control over the cardiovascular-renal diseases, cancer, and accidents. These three causes combined account for more than
three-fourths of all current deaths. But these gains, Dr.
Dublin says, will be limited because mortality from these
causes is concentrated in the latter half of the life span.

John Donne, the seventeenth-century British poet and
dean of St. Paul's, wrote, "Death, thou shalt die." Dramatic
improvements in the quantity and quality of health services
have now decreed, "Death, thou shalt wait." But as Dr.
Dublin points out, the extension of this waiting period will
not be so great in the future as some have predicted.

Contrary to opinions expressed by some, the growing incidence of chronic disability in our nation is a tribute to
American medicine rather than an indictment. But as the
physician has been largely responsible for this development,
he must assume leadership in its solution.

Rehabilitation has frequently been termed the "third
phase of medicine," following "preventive medicine" and
"curative medicine and surgery." It is that period when the
"fever is down and the stitches are out," the period "between the bed and the job." In contrast to "convalescence"
in which the patient is left alone to let nature and time take
their course, rehabilitation is a dynamic concept in which
the skills of the rehabilitation team, consisting of the physicians, physical therapists, occupational therapists, nurses,
social workers, counselors, and other trained personnel, are
integrated together as a single force to assist the patient in
reaching the maximum of his physical, emotional, social, and
vocational potentials.

The first objective of rehabilitation is to eliminate the

physical disability if that is possible; the second, to reduce or alleviate the disability to the greatest extent possible; and the third, to retrain the person with a residual physical disability "to live and to work within the limits of his disability but to the hilt of his capabilities."

One of the most significant medical and social advances of the past decade is the growing interest, both professionally and among the public throughout the world, of the development of rehabilitation services for the physically handicapped. Undoubtedly, much of this interest in expanding rehabilitation opportunities and services for the handicapped has resulted both directly and indirectly from World War II, when attention was focused on the problems of disabled servicemen. Such advances, however, are not entirely due to this impetus, as the growth of rehabilitation services for the handicapped is a part of a total pattern of an expanding community, national, and global consciousness of social welfare which is reflected in similar advances in all educational, health, and social services.

As in all great social movements, this increased interest in rehabilitation has been a result of the impact and recognition of increased needs—in this instance, the rapid increase in the developed parts of the world of the incidence of chronic disability as a result of the increasing age of the population.

Although some nations of the world still have pressing problems of communicable disease, and life expectancy rates vary from nation to nation, depending on the availability of medical care, public health measures, food supply, and the general standard of living, the trend in all nations is toward a greatly increased life expectancy, with the result that throughout the world our population is gradually becoming older.

At the same time that the average age is advancing in the

developed parts of the world, a new concept of the dignity of man and the value of the worth of the individual is beginning to emerge in those nations of the world which do not have the benefits as yet of modern programs of public health and medical care. This new concept of the worth of the individual has been symbolized, and is finding its expression in many instances, in the desire of these nations to institute programs of services for their physically handicapped.

Rehabilitation has been defined as the ultimate restoration of the disabled person to his maximum capacity—physical, emotional, social, and vocational. Implicit in this definition is the need for a team whose members can bring together a wide variety of skills and understandings. No one profession can furnish all the services needed. Rehabilitation is, rather, an area of specialized activity within a number of professional disciplines.

During the thirty-five years I have been in medicine I have seen slow but steady progress toward acceptance of the more enlightened view of physical fitness in terms of ability to perform a specific task. Physical criteria for ability to work were drawn up, in the first and second decades of this century, under the then prevailing "anatomical concept" of medicine. Competency and physical ability were measured in terms of anatomical perfection. A man was either fit or unfit, depending upon whether or not he was anatomically whole.

But times have changed. It is now know physiologically that man can live with one-half of a lung, one-third of a kidney, one sixty-fourth of a liver, one-half of the normal volume of blood, and without a stomach. Although far from whole anatomically, he can function effectively. Thus, under the current physiological or functional concept of medicine, the individual may be physically disabled, but he is not vocationally handicapped if placed in the right job. Few persons use more than one-quarter of their physical capacities in daily living.

The greatest single asset in vocational success of the disabled person is the patient himself and his tremendous powers of recuperation and compensation. The blind man, for example, compensates for the loss of sight by overdeveloping his senses of touch and hearing, for this is now the way he sees.

Among the many great rewards of working closely with my friends and neighbors, the physically handicapped, is the tremendous daily inspiration which I have received from their strength, courage and tolerance. Great ceramics are not made by putting clay into the sun. They come only from the white heat of the kiln. In the firing process, some pieces are broken, but those that survive the heat are transformed from clay into porcelain of great beauty. So it is, it seems to me, with the sick, suffering, and disabled. Those who through medical skills, opportunity, and their own courage survive their illness and overcome their handicap have a depth of spirit and tolerance that can result only from a soul-shaking experience. They have not wasted their pain.

Writing in *The New York Times Sunday Magazine* seven years ago, Arnold Toynbee said, "The twentieth century will be chiefly remembered . . . as an age in which human society dared to think of the welfare of the whole human race as a practicable objective."

One, and perhaps the most significant, feature of social development which gives hope of Mr. Toynbee's objective becoming reality is the increasing recognition throughout the world that the security and welfare of the human race are interdependent within each geographical area of the world and that the security and welfare of each geographical area of the world are dependent on the security and welfare of the world as a whole.

I, for one—and I am sure this concept is shared by the great majority of people in the world regardless of their race, religions, nationalities, or professions—believe this growing recognition of mutual interdependence has not resulted solely from practical necessity. I believe it also represents our ability, as our society matures, to give fuller expressions to a feeling that is as old as mankind itself—to the desire to share with and help one's neighbor.

It has long seemed to me that in the field of health and rehabilitation, we have a uniquely effective area of service and responsibility for working toward international understanding.

In this country and in the other developed parts of the world we have seen a remarkable growth of interest in rehabilitation in the last decade. This interest has not been prompted by humanitarian motives alone. It has resulted from the growing incidence of physical disability resulting from prolongation of the life span, increased public assistance costs because of disability, and our need for manpower in our expanding economy.

But what lies behind the interest of Indonesia, Korea, the Philippines, Mexico, India, Burma, and Thailand in the provision of rehabilitation services for their handicapped? It is not the need for manpower, for these nations have far more manpower than they can profitably utilize in their present stage of industrial development. It is not to reduce public assistance costs, for few of these nations have any social schemes whereby the disabled become a responsibility of the state. It is not to reduce demands for medical, hospital, and social services, for the chronically ill and disabled of most of these nations are wards of their families rather than of the state.

The real reason is that many of these nations, particularly those of the Africa-Asia area, have, after years of colonization, recently achieved the long-sought dream of political independence. Now they are desperately looking for ways of proving to the world, and more importantly to themselves, that they have the political and social maturity to justify their political independence.

Among my friends and neighbors is a youngster from Bolivia named Juanito Yepez. I came to know Juanito through a young doctor whom I met at a medical meeting five years ago who came up to me and said: "I am just back from a teaching mission in Bolivia, and there I saw a wonderful child that I wish could have a chance. He was born without arms and legs. He has four little sensitive fingers that come from each shoulder joint and two normal feet that come from each hip joint. His mother and father are dead. He lives in the mission there and has for the last six years. He is eight years old now. He gets every place by rolling, like a little ball. He is very bright. Could you possibly help him?"

I replied, "I don't see how we can. We have no budget and I don't know how we would get him up here, but send the records and send the pictures; you never can tell."

One day, shortly afterwards, I was late for an appointment with the secretary of a distinguished man. While she sat waiting in my office, she couldn't help but see the case report and the pictures of this child on my desk When I came in, she asked me about this case and I told her the story. She said: "Well, he will come. I have been fortunate in my employment all these years. I have saved my money. I have no family. This child will come and I will adopt him while he is in the United States."

Panagra flew Juanito up and he landed all alone in the world, about three weeks later with two words of English— "please" and "thank you"—and a grin from ear to ear. Two weeks before Juanito arrived, I lunched at the UN with the Vice President, who is now the President, and the Ambassador of Bolivia. They knew about Juanito and they were eager to learn about his plans. In the middle of the lunch I threw the bomb on the table and said, "If we bring this boy up here, it is going to cost you a very large fee"—they winced as I added—"a great fee."

They asked, "What is the fee?" I said: "The fee will be a promise of two things: first, when he returns to your country, he will have the best education your country affords; and, second, if we demonstrate what can be done with the most severely disabled child in the world, you will set up a national rehabilitation center in La Paz." They didn't hesitate a second; they said, "Doctor, you take the boy; we pay the fee."

Juanito is now walking on his fourth set of specially designed prosthesis. He has an electric wheelchair that he can whizz around any place he wants to go; he is in the fifth grade in school—a great child.

Several months after he first came, his story was written up in *Newsweek*. About three weeks later, the editors received a letter postmarked Tampico, Mexico, which read: "Congratulations on a brilliant piece of reporting. Am referring to your article on Juanito Yepez, the congenital quadruple amputee from Bolivia. Those of us in and out of Central and South America found your article on Juanito gained us more friends (and respect) than all the millions our government is pouring into these countries. We noted no sudden pro USA feelings in Brazil as a result of the $75 million donation [given Brazil by the US], but we were pleasantly surprised with the many compliments for what the USA is doing for Juanito. I do not know what your circulation is in Latin America but can tell you the peons in the backwoods knew all about Juanito within 24 hours after the issue was on the streets."

A few years ago my friends and neighbors at the Institute of Physical Medicine and Rehabilitation and I were given a prayer written by an unknown Confederate soldier. We have titled it, "A Creed for Those Who Have Suffered." To us it explains that which is usually unexplainable.

I asked God for strength that I might achieve,
I was made weak that I might humbly learn to obey.
I asked for health that I might do greater things,
I was given infirmity that I might do better things.
I asked for riches that I might be happy,
I was given poverty that I might be wise.
I asked for power that I might have the praise of men,
I was given weakness that I might feel the need of God.
I asked for all things that I might enjoy life,
I was given life that I might enjoy all things.
I got nothing that I asked for—but everything I had hoped for.
Almost despite myself, my unspoken prayers were answered.
I am among all men, most richly blessed.

THE SOCIALLY HANDICAPPED

By DOUGLAS C. RIGG

Those confined behind prison walls
and separated from their families,
their futures uncertain—the socially
handicapped — are "neighbors" to
Douglas Rigg.

DOUGLAS C. RIGG, nationally known forward-looking warden of Minnesota State Prison, was born November 2, 1912 in New Orleans, Louisiana. His family moved to Brooklyn, New York, soon after, and he was raised in that "wonderful" town to which he ascribes his enduring love for baseball.

After graduating from the University of California in 1938, Mr. Rigg studied at the Stanford Graduate School of Business Administration and at the New York School of Social Work. In January, 1941, he joined the prison service of the State of California as San Quentin's first institutional parole officer, and subsequently served as Supervising Parole Officer, Supervisor of Classification, Associate Warden-Classification, and Associate Warden-Custody of that institution. In April, 1955, he was appointed to his present position when he placed first in a nationwide competitive examination for the post.

Mr. Rigg's interests, apart from his work and his family, are sailing, golf, and literature. He has written for the various professional journals in his field and for the *Saturday Evening Post*.

The Socially Handicapped

MY NEAREST neighbors are 1,300 convicts. One of them cooks my family's meals, and another one drives my eleven-year-old daughter to school each morning. 650 of them work in the industries at the Minnesota State Prison where I work as their Warden. Others help to operate our power plant, work in our hospital, cook in our kitchen, or are laundrymen, electricians, brick masons, carpenters, or work in a host of varied occupations required in the operation of a walled city. 210 of my neighbors live beyond the walls to work our farm, man our warehouses, labor at conservation in two nearby State Parks, or run business machines in the Prison Administration Building. Sixty of my neighbors are so dangerous that it is necessary to keep them behind the most secure bars, the most secure locks, the prison has.

Practically all of my neighbors will some day leave the prison, either by parole or by discharge. Even if there were no parole system in my state, there would be little change in

37

the percentage released. Without the use of parole we would probably have to build another penitentiary costing some 12 million dollars because prisoners would serve longer periods. But still, the vast majority would serve out their sentences and go free.

I remember how surprised I was to learn that more than 95 per cent of the country's convicts get out of prison. This fact is no longer new and strange to me, and I hope it is becoming equally familiar to an increasing number of my fellow citizens. If so, then you will agree that the kind of neighbor the ex-convict will be for you depends considerably upon what you permit me to do with him while he is yet a neighbor of mine.

The story of crime and punishment often provides vicarious experience for many of us. We are often chided for our seemingly morbid interest in life outside the law. Crime news, crime fiction, television, and the movies regale us with the tales of the latest unsolved homicide or the thrillers of Mr. Hitchcock. Stanley Hyman, writing of the tragic drama, quotes St. Augustine: "What is the reason that a spectator desires to be made sad when he beholds doleful and tragic passages which he, himself, could not suffer to endure?" Perhaps we see in today's crimes what more fortunate cultures found in Aeschylus and Shakespeare.

Certainly, the whole subject of crime and punishment is dramatic as well as tragic. It is tragic for its victims, for our society, and for our criminals. I can find no great quarrel with our national fascination for the crime scene. It is important enough to demand our attention. What I do regret, rather, is our lack of real knowledge and genuine understanding about it. For example, we are all aware that there is much crime in the United States and that it is costly. But no one knows exactly how much crime there is in our country and how much it costs in dollars and cents, let alone human cost. We are a statistics-minded people from baseball averages to indices of productivity. Private or governmental statisticians keep us informed of almost everything except crime—how much, where, and what? In brief, we have no completely accurate national crime statistics as Mr. Herbert Hoover tells us in a recent issue of *This Week Magazine.* "There remains," he writes, "a vast area of things about crime we don't know. What we don't know is what happens after these crimes are committed. In other words, how efficient are our procedures and methods of justice in stemming this rising flood of crime." Ex-President Hoover acknowledges that the national crime statistics published by the FBI do a good job in showing major crimes, crime trends, and the increase in crime among our young people. But he properly complains that they are still not complete and sees the proper solution to the problem as a crime census to be taken by the United States Census Bureau.

In my job I meet the unsuccessful criminals, people who get caught, tried, convicted, and imprisoned. These are perhaps the men and women we read most about in our newspapers or in our pulp magazines. And they provide the generally accepted and understood picture of the breakers of our laws. They are the burglars, robbers, forgers, murderers, sex offenders, and petty thieves that fill our jails and our prisons. Few of us know much about the successful criminal who seldom sees the inside of a precinct house or courtroom, let alone a prison. Some of them are the white collar criminals, still among us in spite of state laws and the US Securities and Exchange Commission. *Fortune Magazine* (November, 1958), in an article on the work of the SEC, reported: "The number of investigations it conducted into shady security transactions rose from 1325 in fiscal 1957 to 1427 in fiscal 1958 . . . yet, despite all this, the number of queasy stock deals and weird corporate manipulations seems to

mount . . ." Each year these big-time operators manipulate
securities or play the chess of high finance with corporations
at the expense of both investors and consumers.

In spite of Senate hearings and court-appointed monitors,
labor racketeers practice their piracy on captive members
and the public. One may naturally wonder about the promise of new laws under consideration when seemingly adequate old laws have been so ineffective. And labor racketeers
flourish best where dishonest employers see in racket-
dominated unions freedom from "interference from organized labor" or a method of illicit competition with law abid-
ing competitors.

And do any of us really know the power and extent of
other forms of organized crime as exemplified by the Mafia
with its interest in gambling, narcotics, and prostitution?
True, Al Capone went to prison—but for failure to pay his
income tax. True, Frank Costello went to prison—but for
failure to cooperate in answering the questions of a Congressional Committee. And with the rise and fall of individual rackets leaders, one always has the uncomfortable
feeling that if individuals come and go, the organizations
continue to survive.

I have discussed white collar crime and the rackets because they provide a perspective we greatly need in studying the crime picture. Few white collar criminals and few
racketeers are found in the nation's prisons. This does not
mean that our other criminals who usually become our convicts are not a major social problem, for they are. But if all
of our prisoners were to disappear or, better yet, to be completely rehabilitated, crime would still be with us. And, of
course, we must also not ignore the other large, continuing
social problems that help to create some of our convicts.
Racial intolerance, our slums, distressed economic areas, our

neglected schools, are certainly at least partly responsible for many criminal careers.

There are more than 200 thousand felons in our federal and state prisons. The overwhelming majority of them are men, native born and of average intelligence. Perhaps the most significant data about our prisoners (other than the fact that most of them will leave prison) are these two: (1) about half of them have been in prison at least once before; and (2) half of them are very young (in their teens and in their twenties). The presence of so many repeaters in prison would suggest that prison neither changes nor deters criminal behavior. And the presence of so many young people would suggest that their patterns of behavior can yet be changed. Both facts are surely a sobering challenge.

If you have driven past a state penitentiary or visited one, the odds are that you have seen a rather old, grim set of buildings suggesting antiquity. Or if you have seen a newly built penitentiary, still its monolithic construction suggests timelessness. Actually, the prison is a relatively modern institution. Not much more than two centuries ago imprisonment was usually a transitory experience for our felons before trial or before punishment. Flogging, mutilation, transportation, and capital punishment (the latter for some 200 crimes) were the accepted method of handling felons.

The political, economic, scientific, and sociological progress of the nineteenth and twentieth centuries left their mark upon the prison. It became at first a substitute for the harsher punishments and then, later, an institution with possibilities of rehabilitation and reform. Society seemed to want to recognize that those crueler, older methods had failed—and they had—and at the same time to show a willingness to try something different. That something different is what the distinguished historian, Harry Elmer Barnes, calls *the new penology.* Briefly, the new penology holds that crime is learned behavior and so criminals are made, not born, and that the best way to control their crimes is to change their criminal behavior.

The new penology sees the prison as a social institution with a job of protecting society by holding convicted felons in secure custody and making all positive efforts to bring about their rehabilitation. Important parts of the new penology are probation, which is a substitute for imprisonment, and parole, which is an adjunct to imprisonment. The new penology seeks to use various disciplines to achieve its goals, including sound law, medicine, psychiatry, casework, clinical psychology, education including vocational training, religious counseling, and work programs. It would study and diagnose each convict and apply the curative treatment indicated. It would classify all prisoners into relatively homogeneous groups for the purpose of treatment and develop varying programs and varied types of institutions from the maximum security to the honor camp. It recognizes that we do not have all the knowledge to explain completely each criminal career nor to treat each criminal, and so it places a major emphasis upon the need for continued research in these two areas. But its major goal would be to restore to society those criminals who can be treated successfully and to keep under secure restraint those who cannot.

We have noted that the figures on recidivism suggest that the new penology is a failure. If the story were this simple, we would be faced with the disappointing, but definite, re-result of an enlightened experiment. Unfortunately, the new penology has never really been tried. I know of no prison system or institution in the United States that has ever been able to adopt the methods of the new penology in anything but insufficient degree. A few states and the Federal Government have tried, but even those which are recognized as leaders in the field fall far, far short of any real degree of application.

California is a case in point. It has enjoyed a progressive penal law and capable leadership intermittently for half a century and, more specifically, for the past two decades. It makes wide use of prisoner classification and the various professional disciplines. But it is unable to obtain and apply these services in sufficient quantity and quality as evidenced by the fact that its rate of recidivism continues close to 50 per cent. In addition, it suffers from the twin handicaps of seriously overcrowded prisons and extensive idleness among inmates. Indeed, idleness or overcrowding, and frequently both, are the rule rather than the exception in our American penitentiaries and reformatories. I cite California not out of criticism but to indicate the problem faced by an acknowledged leader among our states in the correctional field. In brief, unless and until the new penology has the opportunity to apply its concepts fully, both in quantity and in quality, its promise will continue to remain unfulfilled, and prisons will continue to house a large proportion of repeaters as well as a large number of our youth.

If the new penology has not really been tried, it still has its share of critics. For example, the ex-convict who returns to crime is commonly pointed to as an example of our country-club prisons or of our soft parole laws or of our failure to make punishment stick. In most instances the offender probably was released from a prison where he spent months or years in relative idleness, where there was little or no attempt made to assist him to change his behavior patterns. Either he was discharged outright from prison without a job and sent upon his way, or if he was paroled, it was to the supervision of an overworked, underpaid parole officer who can barely manage to keep superficial contact with his case load of 100 to 300 parolees.

When prisons experience riots and disturbances, our news-paper headlines call for drastic action. Usually an investiga-tion is held, a few heads roll, but seldom are the conditions that breed disturbances essentially changed. It is much simpler to fire a warden or let him resign than to eliminate politics from prison control, to provide adequate staff, to create work for prisoners, to segregate the more dangerous offenders from the rest of the prison population, to establish a treatment program, or to train prison employees for their difficult and important job. Again we are, of course, con-cerned with the drama of crime and punishment, but our concern is that of the spectator who repeatedly views the same play without ever understanding it.

What do I want for my neighbors, who are yours and will be yours again and, too often, mine again? First, I would ask for understanding, an understanding based on knowl-edge rather than on fear. Karl Menninger, America's fore-most psychiatrist, writing in *Harper's Magazine* (August, 1959) declares:

If we were to follow scientific methods, a convicted offender would be detained indefinitely pending a decision as to whether and how and when to reintroduce him successfully into society. All the skill and knowledge of modern behavioral science would be used to examine his personality assets, his liabilities and po-tentialities, the environment from which he came, its effect upon him, and his effects upon it.

Having arrived at some diagnostic grasp of the offender's personality, those in charge can decide whether there is a chance that he can be redirected into a mutually satisfactory adaptation to the world. If so, the most suitable techniques in education, industrial training, group administration, and psychotherapy should be selectively applied. All this may be best done extra-or intra-murally. It may require maximum security or only minimum security. If, in due time, perceptible change occurs, the process should be expedited by finding a suitable spot in society and industry for him, and getting him out of prison control and into civil status (with parole control) as quickly as possible. . . .

There will be some offenders about whom the most experienced are mistaken both ways. And there will be some concerning whom no one knows what is best. There are many problems for research. But what I have outlined is, I believe, the program of modern penology. . . .

It is *our* move. And our move must be a constructive one, an intelligent one, a purposeful one—not a primitive, retaliatory, offensive move. We, the agents of society, must move to end the game of tit-for-tat and blow-for-blow in which the offender has foolishly and entirely engaged himself and us. We are not driven, as he is, to wild and impulsive actions. With knowledge comes power, and with power there is no need for the frightened vengeance of the old penology. In its place should go a quiet, dignified, therapeutic program for the rehabilitation of the disorganized one, if possible, the protection of society during his treatment period, and his guided return to a useful citizenship, as soon as this can be effected.

In spite of serious gaps in our knowledge of criminal behavior, we do have sufficient knowledge and experience to do something intelligent and constructive with our prisoners. As citizens, we must insist that our elected representatives follow a party or personal platform plank expressing the kind of concern for offenders that Dr. Menninger requests. And we will further insist that the plank be backed by the laws and appropriations it needs. We must also insist that our governors appoint qualified personnel to run our correctional institutions and that political interference be relegated as too dangerous and too expensive.

To be even more specific, we will have to accept as necessary and desirable such practical policies as follows:

1. Decent wages for prison and parole employees. The median figure for prison officers is about $3600 annually.

We will have to raise that to $5000 annually to attract and to hold the men capable of doing the job we want done.

2. Work and wages for prisoners.

3. Parole Board members appointed on the basis of professional qualifications, instead of political expediency. We have professional standards for doctors, lawyers, pharmacists, chiropractors, and beauty shop operators. But we have no standards for the men and women who have to make the important decisions as to who get out of prison and when.

4. Reduce parole case loads. A trained parole officer can be effective with a case load of 30. His effectiveness varies inversely as his case load goes up. Experiments with small case loads in New York State and in California have scientifically demonstrated what most intelligent people had already assumed—namely, that with small case loads even the most difficult and less promising offenders can be restored to useful citizenship through parole.

5. Select genuine economy over pseudo economy. Various states have had low-cost prisons and high-cost riots. Small parole case loads are cheaper than prisons. And somewhere, some day, someone will have the good sense to charge the parolee for a portion of his supervision in recognition that we appreciate what we pay for, and to give the parolee the dignity and the responsibility of meeting an increasing number of his personal obligations.

6. Supporting, either through participation or financially, or preferably both, the work of those organizations concerned with effective crime control. Perhaps you are fortunate enough to reside in a state that has a prison society. But where there is no prison society, our service clubs, church groups, and fraternal and women's clubs —all have a proper stake in sound correctional practices

and should be activated to participate in the study and support of such practices. Some four years ago the American Association of University Women in Minnesota studied the state correctional programs. Out of their study came a recommendation for a Prisoner's Aid Society, and this society became a reality. They have also continued to support improved programs as well as necessary changes in the law.

Prisoners tell a wry joke about the prison law. "It is there," they quip, "not to keep us in, but to keep the public out." This, unfortunately, is too often true. And although the public stays on its side of the wall, time eventually makes neighbors of the public and the prisoner. He will again, inevitably, be your neighbor. How good a neighbor depends not upon me but upon you.

THE
NEGLECTED

By DOROTHY DAY

Those really down and out, without
food, clothing, employment, or money,
the poverty-stricken, the seeking, are
"neighbors" to Dorothy Day.

DOROTHY DAY, friend of the poor and forsaken, was born in Brooklyn in 1897. Her father's work as a newspaperman caused the family to move frequently, and her childhood was spent not only in Brooklyn, but also in Chicago and California.

In 1916, after two years at the University of Illinois, she moved to New York where she worked for the New York *Call*, the old *Masses*, and *The Liberator;* and later, for various other newspapers throughout the United States. Activity for the cause of women's suffrage resulted in Miss Day's being jailed for picketing the White House in 1918.

The birth of her daughter, Therese, inspired Dorothy Day to enter the Roman Catholic Church. In 1933, under the direction and tutelage of Peter Maurin, a French peasant, she founded the Catholic Worker movement, which, in addition to its paper with a world-wide circulation of 65,000, has autonomous houses of Hospitality and farms through the country, where all work without salary, hiring, or firing, the uniting bond of the movement being the Works of Mercy.

Although there is diversity of opinion in the movement on the questions of pacifism and anarchism, Dorothy Day's own uncompromising attitude against the modern state and its preparation for war has led her to serve annual jail sentences for refusing to participate in compulsory air raid drills.

In addition to lectures at Harvard, Yale, The New School, Brandeis, and many Roman Catholic and non-Roman Catholic colleges, Miss Day has written four books —*From Union Square to Rome, On Pilgrimage, House of Hospitality,* and *The Long Loneliness*—as well as many magazine articles and short stories.

The Neglected

---

*E*VERY CITY has its skid row, and the term probably came from the Northwest among the lumbermen who found it hard to keep their balance when they arrived in the cities after long, hard work in the solitudes. The Bowery is the Skid Row of New York, and it extends from Cooper Union on the north to Chatham Square on the south. To the west are the southern reaches of Greenwich Village and, south of that, Little Italy, and to the east, the great teaming, steaming East Side.

From the time I first went to work for the New York *Call* at the age of eighteen, I have called the East Side home, and whenever I came back from periods of stay in the Middle West, I always returned to it. Here, on the East Side, I was first introduced to radicalism; and my early interest in unions stemmed from my contact with the East Side Russian and Polish Jews, whose many meetings I attended during the days of conflict between the A F of L craft unions and the Amalgamated Clothing Workers. Working on radical

51

papers meant living with the poor in their tenements, and
in those days a tenement was a four-room apartment, one
room with a door on the hall which could be rented out
while the family of six or eight lived in the other three rooms.
There was a toilet in the hall and a bathtub by the sink, and
the lodger could use the public baths in the neighborhood.
Today the conditions remain the same—only worse. The
four-room apartments have been chopped up into two-room
apartments; and under pressure of law and the inspection
of city agencies, there are hot water and better toilet facilities, but the rents have been raised accordingly. So the poor,
the Puerto Ricans, the Negroes, are living in ever more
crowded quarters, many driven with their large families to
housekeeping in one-room.

These are the poor whom I love, and they are easy to love,
with their beautiful children, with their hard-working parents, with their striving for education, and better health and
living conditions. It is not so easy to love the poor of the
skid rows, of the Bowery, and yet that is where our work
has led us.

When I say "us" I mean the group associated with *The
Catholic Worker,* an eight page tabloid published monthly
with a circulation of 65,000, which goes all over the country,
and even to countries throughout the world. "The Catholic
Worker is not an organization," Peter Maurin, its founder,
used to say. "It is an organism." Yes, a dynamic organism
that grows, that spreads, that has life. It has been that because the young people who have made up its staff over the
26 years of its existence have come to it with ideals, with
a longing for utopia, with the hopeful conviction that even
now one can begin to make the kind of society where it is
easier for people to be good. And when they fell in love and
married, or found other vocations in honorable occupations,
they were like seeds scattered across the country. Soon other

young people came to take their places. And thus has the movement lived.

Peter Maurin was a follower of Peter Kropotkin, the philosopher-anarchist who wrote *Mutual Aid,* and *Fields, Factories, and Workshops.* He was a follower of Jefferson, who taught personal responsibility and wrote, "He governs best who governs least." He was a follower of St. Francis, who stood for voluntary poverty and the freedom that goes with it. He was a follower of Eric Gill, the artist and writer, also a pacifist and anarchist, and of Chesterton and Belloc, who were Distributists. He was a great teacher and brought us the writings of Don Luigi Sturzo, and Frs. Tomkins and Coady of Nova Scotia; of Karl Adam of Germany; and of Maritain, Peguy and Leon Bloy of France. He made for us a synthesis of cult, culture, and cultivation, as he called it, and that made up the "Green Revolution."

The Catholic Worker group was founded on the principle of voluntary poverty, which means that no one gets a salary and that all goods are held in common. We are a community living in hospices, trying to answer the calls made on us to feed the hungry, shelter the harborless, clothe the naked, etc. In fact, our rule in life *is* the works of mercy—the seven corporal and the seven spiritual works. The former are listed in the twenty-fifth chapter of St. Matthew, and there is no excuse permitted by our Lord for not following them. "When did we see you hungry and not feed you, in prison and not visit you?" And the reply is firm, "If you have done these things to the least of these my brethren, you have done them unto me." Ruskin wrote about these works in *Unto This Last,* and when Gandhi read the essay on a train in South Africa, it did much to change his life.

For the first few years of the Catholic Worker's existence we were located in an old East Side house where we had rented several apartments for offices, and nearby we found a few other apartments for living quarters. We tried to answer each need as it came. For one year we located in a house on the West Side. Then one of our readers offered us the use of an unused rear tenement, two blocks off the Bowery, and for the next 15 years we found ourselves identified with work for the most neglected and the least loved of all the poor—the alcoholics, the aged, the crippled of Skid Row.

Dwight McDonald said once that our work was caring for the undeserving poor. We had thought to be sure, that we would be working for social justice, for better legislation, better institutions, for unionization of workers—in other words, for a dignified cause; but the leadership of a little French peasant, Peter Maurin, brought us to the down and outs, to those called bums, to the lame, the halt, and the blind, to the disorderly poor. There was no honor, no dignity in the work, either for them or for us. To speak in this way is to look at men in the mass and that, of course, is not the way to look at them. You have to take them one by one. I can call these brothers of ours the most neglected because, humanly speaking, they are the least respected. "Give money to bums who will drink it all up? Contribute to their delinquency by feeding, clothing, and sheltering them so to enable them to live without working?" This was the judgment so often passed on our work—yes, this and even harsher judgments. We were even accused of a perverse love of filth and disorder, and of being drawn to these scenes of human misery by a desire to "seek the downward path which leads to salvation," as Baudelaire put it.

I can only say that this work is a constant exercise of our faith, which is born of our desire to see Christ in our brother—in his most hidden guise. It is the Gospels themselves which have brought us to this work, because Jesus is left to us in the poor, as well as in the Eucharist, and as well

as on those occasions when "two or three are gathered together" in his name. A priest once told us that a weightlifter
exercises and practices each day by lifting a few more
ounces until his burden becomes gigantic and yet he can
bear it. It is so with our work. Each day we seek Christ in
his poor, and in each encounter we have an opportunity to
find him.

Our headquarters now is a huge loft, 175 feet deep, by 50
feet wide, on the third and top floor of a building on Spring
Street, between Mott and Mulberry Streets. We face the
south, with windows on three sides so that we have air as
well as space. Across the street is a playground full of children and their mothers, and at tables to one side a few old
men playing chess. There is a fountain in the center, which
is turned on several times a day for the children to cool
off under its pleasant spray. As always in the slums, people
sit on the streets, in front of their houses which remain hot
and airless long after a heat wave has passed.

Our loft is reached by two long flights of stairs, but that
does not keep people from coming to us all day. Probably
about fifty people use this long loft, divided into dining
room and office and clothes room, as a day shelter. At one
side men shave at a small sink. At the far end there is a large
stove on which there are always pots of soup or stew or
hash and macaroni and cheese baking in the oven. Today
there is with us, a man with his leg in a cast, and near him
a middle-aged woman soaking her swollen foot. She does
this three or four times a day, keeping the pan under her
chair. Nearby an old woman is braiding a rug out of the silk
ties which came to us in gift boxes of clothes. There are
some reading, some sleeping, head on chest, even as they
sit upright. There are even some stretched out on a few
chairs or in the corner on the floor, taking a nap. We who
work and live in these surroundings lose sight of the fact

that these are strange sights, as grotesque and moving in their way as the lithographs of Kathe Kollwitz.

But the fact of the matter is that this headquarters of the Catholic Worker group is a home, and people feel at home and feel that they belong. On the wall over the table there is a wooden crucifix, painted green, which crosswise reads, *Love God*, and lengthwise, *Do What You Will*. To "love God and do what you will," of course, means, as St. Augustine wrote it, that this is the liberty of Christ: when you love God, your will follows God's will.

Over on the Bowery, two blocks away, men are sleeping in doorways because the big Municipal Lodging House has become a jungle where the stabbings, muggings, and beatings are such that men are afraid to go there unless they are fortified with plenty of that cheap Bowery wine that can be bought for thirty-five cents a pint. To them it is preferable to sleep in the open rather than go to such a place. So these warm nights and days, the homeless sleep on the streets. Of course, police vans go around and pick them up and cart them to the Tombs for overnight. Sometimes they are dismissed the next morning; at other times, when there is a clean-up campaign on, they are sentenced to Rikers Island or Hart's Island or to one of the other prisons.

When one of our family, one who clings to the Catholic Worker group in an effort to get back on his feet, disappears for a few days, we know that he has been picked up in one of these periodic police clean-ups. One of our men, Hugh, who dresses like a tramp and likes to go barefoot most of the summer, was picked up just the other day and kept for a few days. Yet he is a most holy tramp, going to Mass daily, reciting the Angelus wherever he is, eating sparingly, working daily. Today he has removed some of the windows on the side of the loft and is replacing the cords so that they will open and shut more easily. And periodically, he will

wash the windows and the stairs and do other such chores
to make the place more homelike. Where hundreds come
and go each day, it is hard for the poor to keep clean.

We do not ask questions at the Catholic Worker because
we feel that we need to show respect for others and trust
them. But we get acquainted little by little. We know each
other by our first names, and it is only when a man is sick
and has to go to the hospital that we realize with a shock that
we do not know the last name of our friend who has been
living with us and eating by our side for many years. But
when we do get to know each other, we realize how unique
each personality is.

How many of us are there? Right now about fifty sit down
to three meals a day, and many more come in for clothes to
fit themselves out for jobs. We have four apartments in the
neighborhood, but only a few men and women can be ac-
commodated there. We pay many other rents, for single
people, for disturbed people, for people who have lost jobs
and have to wait weeks to get their unemployment insurance. We put many men up on the Bowery and women
in the Salvation Army home or the Jeanne D'Arc residence.
Altogether we spend about eight hundred dollars a month
in rents. It is amazing how many we can care for with so
little. As fast as money goes out (if we spend it without
question), it comes in, in small amounts, from the readers
of our paper, and from the appeals we make twice a year.
(We have to give an accounting of these two begging letters
and their results to some State department in Albany,
following legislation which tries to protect people from
fraudulent appeals. But we will never be anything else but
poor, and our books are open to all.)

In addition to our work in New York City, we have
a little 23-acre farm on Staten Island, and two small beach
bungalows at Raritan Bay, also on Staten Island. Here we

take care of those who need rest from the city, and here we
have Sunday afternoon conferences to discuss the theory of
the "Green Revolution."

And what are some of these theories that are so hard to
write about in the small space of this essay on the poor? We
know that the poor we will always have with us, but we
are not content that there should be so many of them. Of
course, there will always be men who drink and who are
crippled mentally, morally, and physically. But we believe
that all men want God, whether they know it or not. All
men seek happiness and well-being and companionship,
which means breaking bread with others, but often the only
way they find it is on Skid Row.

But if we believe that all men are made in the image and
likeness of God, and think of God as creator—and man,
too, as a creator—then we see this man for the frustrated
creature he is. He is unemployed not only because of the
great advances in technology, but also because he has
cracked up under the pressure of the industrial system
under which we live. Yet work is as necessary to a man as
bread.

Yesterday I was talking to a real craftsman, a furniture
finisher, who loves the material he works with and always
has plenty of work. He expresses himself in his work and
finds joy in his labor. He came to spend his vacation with
us because he loved Peter Maurin's ideas and wanted to
teach such crafts as chair-caning to some of our unemployed.
When he spoke of "caressing" the wood he was polishing, I
remembered that Fr. Jean de Menasce had, in an article
about the sex obsessions of Americans, observed that a good
part of the reason for that obsession lay in the fact that
Americans had no joy in their work—that they were not
able to satisfy their creative urge in the work of their hands.

There are missions on the Bowery doing good and noble

work among the poor, but there are never enough because
thousands are falling by the wayside because of drink, drugs,
unemployment or overwork, mental and physical illnesses.
Many who could be employed are not employed because of
the fears of good people—fear of financial loss if they
employ epileptics and former mental patients, or the ruptured and crippled. We have been working now for over
twenty-six years, and housing conditions now are worse than
ever, and the increasing numbers of old people increase the
total number of the poor. We have not solved the problem
of poverty, the problems of the city slums, of the skid rows.

But there are ways, if we would look for little ways to the
Gospel and literally apply the words of Jesus: "Blessed
are the poor." "Let him who has two coats give to him who
have none." "When you have guests for your feast, invite the
stranger, not your relatives and friends," and so on.

There are very many other aspects of our work having
to do with man's freedom and his responsibility. As follow-
ers of Christ, we believe that he set us an example when he
washed the feet of his disciples and told them—and us—
to do likewise. For us that means literally that we should
try to take the least place. We believe in authority which
is earned and deserved, and our men who cook have authority in the kitchen and the man who farms has authority
on the land. One worker yesterday said, "We have no bosses
—we are a group working together."

Our literal acceptance of the Gospel leads us to pacifism,
a pacifism which does not allow us to vote, serve on juries,
judge others, or condemn them to death. It has brought us
to jail when we would not participate in what we consider
to be "war games" rather than valid attempts to save life in
Civil Defense drills. Going to jail each year for the last five
years has meant that we were performing the work of mercy
of visiting the prisoner.

Our work, which looks on the surface to be a grim and hopeless one very often, is truly a joyful one however, because we can say with St. Augustine:

Who truly rejoices unless he loves the good which is the source of his joy? Who can have real peace unless he has it with him whom he truly loves? Who is sufficiently patient to continue to persevere in good work unless he is fervent in love? Who is kind unless he loves the one he is aiding? Who is good unless he is made so by loving? Who is sound in faith if he lacks the faith which works through love? Who can be mild to any great extent unless he is tempered with love? Who can be continent from that which is shameful unless he loves that which ennobles? With good reason then the Master insists upon love so often as though love alone should be prescribed as the grace without which no other is of avail; without which no one can have the other good things which make a man truly good.

So we pray daily that God will teach us that love which makes all work light. We want to grow in the love of God, by seeing Christ in each one who comes to us, especially in all these neglected ones on our skid rows.

THE
ALCOHOLIC

By EBBE CURTIS HOFF

Those who seek through alcohol to escape from their deeper problems are "neighbors" to Ebbe Hoff.

EBBE CURTIS HOFF, long active in the field of alcoholism, is professor of Neurological Science and dean of the School of Graduate Studies of the Medical College of Virginia in Richmond, Virginia. He is Medical Director of the State Health Department's Division of Alcohol Studies and Rehabilitation in the Medical College of Virginia Hospital.

Dr. Hoff was born in Kansas and grew up in the State of Washington, where he received the Bachelor of Science degree from the University of Washington in Seattle. He holds the degrees of Master of Arts, Doctor of Philosophy, and Doctor of Medicine from Oxford University, England, and was for some years a research fellow and instructor at Yale University School of Medicine.

Dr. Hoff has been a member, since its inception, of the Committee on Society and Alcohol of the Department of Christian Social Relations of the Protestant Episcopal Diocese of Virginia, and a member of the Joint Commission on Alcoholism of the Church's National Council.

The Alcoholic

IN THE Autumn of 1946, I came to the Medical College of Virginia in Richmond to develop a laboratory of experimental neuro-physiology. War years in the Navy had interrupted a train of investigations aimed at an understanding of the processes whereby the central nervous system, especially at its higher levels in the cerebral cortex, exercises jurisdiction over the visceral functions of the body —such as the regulation of heart, circulation, alimentary tract, and secretory glands.

These studies, begun earlier at Yale University, I had pursued with the hope—by no means original with me—of casting some light upon the mysterious way in which living organisms, and specifically human beings, have achieved this integrated functioning which has been expressed as mind-brain or psychosomatic action. In particular, I was concerned with central regulation of the autonomic nervous system—that system of nerves which takes part in the control of heart, blood vessels, endocrine and other glands, and the automatic or semi-automatic workings of the muscle of gut, excretory, and reproductive tracts. How are these functions coordinated with the exquisitely balanced movements of our skeletal musculature? All this seemed a promising point of research because of a well-known relationship of autonomic disturbances and emotional disorders. It appeared worth-while to provide a physiological model (or at least parts of such a model) that would help us to understand how alarm, fear, anxiety, aggression, hostility, sexual passion and other feelings are experienced in terms of the pounding heart, the redirection of the coursing blood, its mounting or falling pressure in the arteries, waves of contraction in the viscera or their inhibition, the inpouring of hormones into the blood, and the outpouring of secretions from the glands of the skin and digestive duct.

This continues to be a promising approach to our understanding of our own natures and is one which is engaging the minds of many workers. My own engagement with these questions persists, and I mention it only because it led me to a commitment to the problems of alcoholism which is the subject of this chapter. Victims of compulsive use of alcohol usually exhibit remarkably sensitive autonomic responses to stresses. In the course of my work, therefore, I found myself from 1946 to 1948 supplementing the investigations in the animal laboratory by study of the autonomic responses of patients whom I was seeing in the neuro-psychiatric clinic and many of whom were alcoholics.

In April, 1948, there was established by an act of the Virginia General Assembly a division of Alcohol Studies and Rehabilitation, to be administered within the framework of the State Health Department with its clinical facilities centered in the Medical College of Virginia. This was not the first state alcoholism program to be established. It was, in fact, one of the practical expressions of a new, growing concern for the plight of the alcoholic which, in great measure, had its modern beginnings in the foundation and growth of Alcoholics Anonymous and the pioneer work of the Yale Center of Alcohol Studies. The Virginia plan was, however, the first state program established within a state health department and organized as a part of a medical teaching and research center. Mr. Kenneth F. Lee, who accepted the directorship of the program, brought to his new task the experience of years in professional rehabilitation work in the State Department of Education. Under his leadership the project was to develop basic research and a plan for the voluntary therapy of patients, utilizing specialized hospital settings and involving long-term outpatient continuation treatment. Such was the program I joined at its inception in October, 1948. We had much to learn. At first, there was but a small outpatient clinic at the Medical College of Virginia. Then in the spring of 1949, we opened a 12-bed inpatient service. Now, although the program is still modest, there are inpatient facilities both at the Medical College of Virginia in Richmond and the University of Virginia Hospital in Charlottesville as well as six active outpatient clinics located throughout Virginia.

These years of research and contact with these ill people in great need have taught us much. There is still more to learn. For one thing, we must revise the common stereotype of the alcoholic. It is tempting to think of alcoholics as characteristically the hopeless, aimless, homeless vagrants of the back alley—the "skid row" denizen, the itinerant, police-court inebriate. Yet probably not more than 8 or 10 per cent of all alcoholics belong in this group. Actually it appears that there may be some four million "problem drinkers" in the United States. Most of these are "hidden" alcoholics—people you don't recognize as such when you see them on the street, in the bus, or in church. They are

young mothers living in new suburban developments, farmers, clerks, skilled workers, salesmen, teachers, businessmen,
doctors, dentists, clergymen, laborers—every kind of
people, rich, poor, educated, and uneducated. They are your
neighbors, your friends, your relatives. There are few people
in America who do not have in their family some member
who is or has been addicted to the pathological use of
alcohol. Alcoholism has become a most democratic affliction;
it has penetrated like a malignant growth into virtually
every part of our socio-cultural structure.

Perhaps it is partly for this reason that one detects a
change in public attitudes towards alcoholism and the problems of alcoholics and their families. The figure of the
"comic" drunk is not quite as funny as he used to be and
one may look forward to the time when a joke about alcoholism will be in as bad taste as a joke about cancer.

This is happening because we are beginning to understand a little better what alcoholism is. It now becomes
more clear that alcoholics are a large group of ill people—
probably not all ill in the same way—who suffer in common from a compulsive use of alcohol which they are powerless to control within normal limits. This phenomenon is
more complex than popular opinion of a few generations
ago appeared to hold. Even the terms, "inebriate," "drunkard," "dipsomaniac," or "alcoholic" are inadequate since
they seem to imply the unrealistic simplification that the
condition is primarily or solely caused by the alcohol or
that it is chiefly described in terms of drinking and drunken
behavior. Hopefully we shall make such progress in our
understanding that new terms will emerge that will recognize that the alcoholic is a sick person who cannot ever
control his drinking by "will power" but that he needs
skillfully planned therapy; that his drinking and drunkenness are symptomatic of illness and therefore are of a

different character and moral order from the inebriety and
alcoholic gluttony of people who are not alcoholics. Alcohol
is a contingent rather than primary cause of the illness of the
alcoholic.

What, then, is alcoholism? First of all, it is a chronic progressive disorder, the victims of which follow a downhill
course. They are increasingly harmed by alcohol. Many—
probably most—alcoholics suffer from prior underlying
psycho-social pathologies, and there is likelihood of some
causative metabolic defect as well. Alcoholics drink excessively—that is, in excess of, and in a pattern deviant
from, the accepted standards of the culture in which they
live. More than this, there is a loss of control of the use of
alcoholic beverages. The inability of the user to drink
moderately is the beginning of addiction. An alcoholic not
only loses control after a few drinks but finds himself often
unable to control the drinking occasion. He may go to a
party planning to remain abstinent and yet the end of the
evening finds him deeply intoxicated.

This loss of control and this compulsive feature of the
alcoholic's condition is mysterious. Some alcoholics go on to
a heavy drinking episode the very day they "take the first
drink." Others may "nip along" for many days or even weeks
before they find themselves in the grips of a devastating
spree or "bender." The latter alcoholic's plight is sometimes
the more perilous since he may be lulled into a false sense
that at last he can drink "normally." He may have maintained abstinence for several months and then starts again
with "a few beers," or "a drink or two" and finds to his
delight that he does not get drunk. It is, however, only a
matter of time before he is back in the grips of his addiction,
as sick as ever. Actually, an alcoholic deludes himself in
looking for a pattern of "moderate" drinking. The mild use
of alcoholic beverages of the so-called moderate drinker has

really no attraction to the alcoholic who, in fact, makes far greater and different demands upon his drink than the moderate user. For some alcoholics the degree of control varies. This week he may seem to get away with a few drinks; next week his drinking goes completely out of hand. Moreover, alcoholism is a progressive pathological process, symptoms becoming more severe, new symptoms recruited, behavior becoming more disorganized, and psychological and organic damages more seriously manifest.

Most alcoholics drink to try to achieve a kind of "glow," a persistent state of tranquility, detachment, or softening of hard reality. They would like to prolong this experience indefinitely, but this proves impossible. Too often the tranquil glow is succeeded by a desperate battle to fight off sickness with more alcohol, which now becomes a medicine to ward off tremors, convulsions, hallucinations, or delirium.

Some alcoholics find it difficult to recognize their condition as such, because their pattern of pathological drinking has never included drinking to the point of a drunken coma. I have known many such patients who have drunk excessively and harmfully for years and yet who assert sincerely that they have never been drunk. These patients drink constantly—a pint to a fifth of whiskey each day, year in and year out. Their drinking is associated with progressive physical and mental deterioration and personality disorganization, and yet such people cannot accept that they are alcoholics because to them the only acceptable stereotype of an alcoholic is a person who becomes staggering drunk and goes on sprees. The alcoholic with the daily pattern may and does pride himself that he can keep going, that he is never noticeably drunk. Actually he is never really sober. His type must be kept in mind when we speak of "loss of control of drinking" as a factor in the definition of alcoholism.

All alcoholics are harmed in some way in the course of

their illness. This harm may be physical in the form of brain damage, liver dysfunction, or other bodily disorder. There may be psychological damage, loss of effectiveness at work, failure of community and social participation and family trouble. A person faced with the need to decide whether or not he is an alcoholic has real difficulty in determining what level of physiological, psychological, and socio-spiritual damage he will recognize and accept as "harm to him." This is the experience of "hitting bottom." How far down must an alcoholic go before he realizes he is powerless over alcohol? How, if at all, can we help him to discover this before he is deteriorated beyond salvage? We do not fully know. Nor do we know exactly the way by which alcohol may be the "cause" of this harm. Just what is the role of alcohol in cirrhosis of the liver or brain disorders? Is it true that in many alcoholics their pathological drinking is a result, a manifestation of some progressive psychological and/or metabolic disturbance? Does alcoholism ever arise *de novo* from heavy "social" drinking? Are there several kinds of alcoholism with different causative patterns? There are reasons to say "yes" to all these three latter questions.

Perhaps the alcoholic finds it so difficult to see clearly his own downhill course and check it because his drink (often from the first) has meant much more to him than ever alcohol has meant to others. The alcoholic finds the effects of alcohol unusually interesting and satisfying. Now, all people, whether alcoholics or not, are affected by taking alcohol into their body. Alcohol, like ether, is anesthetic. It is quite quickly absorbed from the alimentary tract (since it needs no digestion) and circulates in the blood. The alcohol is distributed by the blood to all parts of the body, including the brain, where it causes changes in mood, feelings, and behavior that may range from a mild sense of relaxation, tranquility, and "lift" to advanced intoxication and drunkenness. In low blood concentrations the alcohol, by its anesthetic action upon higher brain cells, releases inhibitions and frees one from anxieties before there is any appreciable deterioration on the sensory or motor or coordinating abilities. This is why alcohol is sometimes spoken of as a "stimulant." Actually, what is happening is that as the blood alcohol concentration rises, successive levels of the central nervous system are becoming temporarily more active until they in turn are put to sleep by the alcohol.

As I have said, all people are affected in this general way by taking alcohol to drink, and any person will become drunk if he drinks enough. People differ individually in the amount of alcohol it takes to produce a certain level of effect, and the same person may be differently affected at different times and under different circumstances. But the reason most people who drink do so (and about 65 million people in the United States do) is to experience mildly or to a greater degree the changes of feeling and mood associated with the stepwise action of alcohol upon the brain. Many people who do not drink at all abstain because they do not care for this effect, or because they find satisfying social, psychological, and other stimuli other ways, or because they find that alcohol makes them feel anxious, insecure, or uncomfortable. Many conscientious people abstain from alcoholic beverages for one or more of the following reasons:

1. They may dislike or be disinclined to experience the effects of alcohol even in mild degrees.
2. Some may conclude that since the use of alcohol does involve certain risks to health (one of which may be becoming an alcoholic later on), such risk is wisely avoided by abstention.

3. Some abstain for economic reasons with the conviction that alcohol is a luxury that may be foregone.

4. Some abstain for occupational reasons—as a physician, aircraft pilot or the clergyman—to insure optimum physical, mental, and emotional efficiency.

5. Some abstain as a considerate self-discipline to support, encourage, and uphold a person such as an alcoholic who cannot safely drink even moderately. (It is well to bear in mind that this motive does not always work. An alcoholic is not necessarily helped by the abstinence of others around him and sometimes may feel that his family practices abstinence as an act of self-righteousness and as a rebuke to him.)

6. Some abstain for sincere humanitarian motives. Many such people honestly believe that the use of alcohol is harmful in our modern society (for example, a danger in driving motor vehicles and operating other modern machinery) and by their own practice and conduct wish to set a positive example of sobriety through abstinence.

7. Finally, some people abstain—temporarily or permanently —for devotional reasons, as some practice fasting or deny themselves in other ways—not because they believe alcohol is "bad" or necessarily harmful, but as an act of special devotion to God.

Many thoughtful people accept the theological position that alcohol—like all of God's creation—is good and that it is possible to practice the virtue of sobriety in either of two ways: (1) through abstinence or (2) through the moderate use of alcoholic beverages. Jesus perfectly exemplified this virtue in the latter way, using bread, wine, and indeed all things to the glory of God and giving thanks to God.

In America, a majority of adults—and many adolescents—

use alcohol to some extent. Since most who drink believe
that they have control over their practice, and since many
who do not drink consider drinking a "habit" which can be
regulated or abandoned by conscientious exercise of "will
power," there is a widespread failure to understand the plight
of the alcoholic. My own experience in discussing this matter
with intelligent people has been to discover their perplexed
incredulity that an alcoholic should go on with his excessive
drinking knowing that it is bringing ruin down around him.
Such a person, it is felt, must be self-indulgent, depraved,
or a psychopathic personality to go on with such a "habit" at
the expense of his health, his position, and the welfare of
his family. It would seem so simple that once he understands
the realities of his situation, he should exercise his will to
break his evil habit and learn to drink normally or not at all.

Our difficulty is that we judge other people's failures in
the light of our own successes. It is hard for a person who
makes little or no demand upon alcohol as a psychological
drug and who gets little or nothing from alcohol to understand that an alcoholic is far from indulging in a "bad habit"
but is actually the victim of a compulsion which inexorably
takes over his life and destroys it. To an alcoholic, his drink
has become the central factor around which his life moves,
without which he cannot face the present at all. Alcohol to
him is not only a stressful agent that tears down his life, it
is also the means by which he tries to adjust to, and cope
with, life. It is for this reason that the rehabilitation of alcoholics is so difficult and requires such skilled therapy; there
is no "cure" for the alcoholic in the sense of restoring him
to "normal" drinking (if indeed he ever did drink normally).
Somehow, he must experience the deep, vivid, sustained inner conviction that he is really powerless over alcohol and
that his life will become increasingly intolerable if he uses
it. Then there must somehow grow within him a sense that

his own life is worth reclaiming and that his own voluntary abstinence is essential to his health and effectiveness. His motivation for abstinence becomes something he values for his own sake and not, for example, something he tries to achieve to prove himself or to offer as a gift to someone he loves. He begins to realize that abstinence is not just "fighting the bottle" by the dogged use of his will but is rather a matter of becoming the kind of person who no longer needs to drink. Thus he comes to respect the seriousness of his illness and to realize that to become rehabilitated he needs help—including skilled, professional therapy (and on a long-term, continuing basis), just as if he had diabetes or a cancer. Our experience in the Virginia program has been that these are the steps taken by those of our patients who now lead abstinent lives. Something of how this happens I shall try to indicate a little later in this chapter.

If non-alcoholics find it hard to understand what is wrong with an alcoholic, may we not also conceive how difficult an alcoholic finds it to understand that he, himself (or she, herself), is ill and in need of outside help. Alcoholics, too, are often victims of the common stereotype of the "drunkard" as a hopeless, shifting vagrant or a social misfit. They, too, think they ought to be able to "drink normally" as their friends do, and that if only they were not so "weak-willed" they could do it. For an alcoholic to accept his condition is sometimes impossible because this would mean characterizing himself according to the popular misconceptions about alcoholics. Thus he would have to accept himself as especially depraved, especially sinful, especially unreliable, and especially unworthy.

My own practice with our patients has suggested that the alcoholic, before he comes to therapy, is a perplexed human being. Alcohol means so much more in his life than it does for non-alcoholics, and yet he tries to operate upon the pat-

tern or model which he observes in non-alcoholics or which
he believes worked for him in past years. What, then, are
some of the motivations which lie behind the conventional
use of alcohol by so-called non-alcoholics?

The drinking of alcoholic beverages is a practice that has
deep roots in cultural heritages, and traditional motives for
their use are strongly embedded in society. Special occasions
—baptisms, weddings and business agreements—are celebrated in the cup. Also, there is a "gourmet" motive in alcohol use, based upon the concept that alcoholic drinks are a
part of gracious living. The hostess who entertains at dinner
with her best table linen, candlelight, and silver may serve
wine and other alcoholic drinks with the same concern for
esthetics as in her service of food to her guests. Moreover,
alcohol may be viewed as an adjunct to social relations.
Social drinking should be defined as that use of alcoholic
beverages that promotes interrelationship between people.
Much so-called "social drinking" fails to meet this definition
when (through the use of alcohol in groups) communication breaks down, the "noise" level rises, and confusion takes
over. This kind of immoderate drinking has a certain appeal
to many who apparently are not alcoholics in the sense that
we are using this term here. We live in times when busy,
harassed people feel the need to tranquilize themselves,
to unwind with alcohol. Going a step further, many like
from time to time to get away from their diligent engagement with ever-present affairs of daily living and live it up,
let down the barriers, and regress.

Finally, in our thinking about motivations for alcohol use,
a word may be said for its prestige appeal. From ancient
times, alcohol comes to us as a symbol and means of life,
strength, and insight into truth: *in vino veritas*. It is not by
accident that drinking has become an acknowledged badge
of accomplished, sophisticated, independent adulthood for

many adolescents. To be able to hold one's liquor is still a hallmark of acceptability in many social groups.

The alcoholic must abandon these motives and, indeed (so far as we know now), cannot look forward ever to drink safely again. The general principles of how his therapy can be effectively carried out must now occupy our attention. First of all, therapy will always be best based upon an understanding of what is wrong with the patient—that is, upon diagnosis and classification. The etiologies and metabolic, psychological, and sociological dynamics of alcoholism are not adequately understood, and yet progress is being made. Research is under way to try to answer such questions as: are there specific characteristics of alcoholics? In the present state of our knowledge there is no specific, standard "cure" of alcoholism, but there are developing some implications for special approaches to these patients. For example, referral and the manner of entry into therapy are particularly important. Often a patient reaches a physician and thence a hospital mainly because the frantic family wants to be rid of the alcoholic or seeks a respite from him. Traditionally, alcoholics have tended to enter therapy during a period of intoxication or in the withdrawal phase of a serious drinking episode. It has even been held that an alcoholic is more than usually accessible to long-term help at such times. This has not necessarily proven true; the patient has sought immediate relief but upon "feeling better" after acute care, a spurious confidence that he could now do it on his own often asserted itself, and he disappeared not to return until the next binge. It is this recidivism that is so discouraging to physicians and other professional people.

The care of the acutely intoxicated patient and the patient in the withdrawal state is important (and many advances have been made in this field), but this is not enough. Effective rehabilitation of alcoholics is not accomplished by

episodic, intermittent, or unplanned treatment. Ongoing
therapy is essential.

We do not fully know just when and under what circumstances an alcoholic is most accessible—most "ready" for
effective rehabilitation. It appears that therapy undertaken
voluntarily is most likely to succeed, and yet no alcoholic
is completely "voluntary"; there is a balance (and/or conflict) between his needs for his drug and his recognition of
the personal deteriorations alcohol inflicts upon him. We
understand alcoholics rightly, I believe, if we assume that
no alcoholic really *wants* to stop drinking; those who finally
get well begin by acknowledging that they *must* do so,
which is a different thing.

For many, motivation for therapy is based upon a new
clarity of insight that alcohol is no longer a satisfying solution. A recognition coming with the force of overwhelming
conviction of one's powerlessness over alcohol can enhance
depression and yet, rightly acted upon, can be the start of
an entirely new way of life. Recognition that in addition to
one's powerlessness over alcohol, one has also been failing
to face daily living even when sober is likewise a devastating
insight, but one which can help orient an alcoholic toward
positive action in planning for a life without alcohol. This
is not just fighting the bottle; there is a new life to learn
how to live.

Traditionally, alcoholics first enter therapy during or just
following an alcoholic drinking episode. The pattern is
drinking, succeeded by acute illness, relief care, recovery
from this disorganized state (with remorse, and good intentions); then follows a sense of release and recovery with
present well-being and a conviction that one needs no further
help. Basic ongoing therapies are rejected; the basic, underlying pathological processes (whatever they are) re-assert

themselves and there is another relapse to drinking with the cycle starting all over again. In our Virginia Division, we are finding that an increasing number of patients are breaking this pattern by first applying for therapy while in alcoholic remission (i.e., when sober) and by regular outpatient clinic treatment on a long-term basis.

Sound therapy for alcoholics (as for all ill people) requires careful diagnosis of the patient's problems and pathologies as well as his resources and assets. In our program, treatment begins with thorough appraisal of medical, family, social, psychological, and psychiatric problems in which a team of internists, social workers, psychologists, and psychiatrists takes part as may be indicated. The new patient is not hit with all this at once, but examination proceeds as he is able to take it. Members of the family, employers, ministers, or others concerned are brought into the picture—and all this with the patient's cooperation. Job and other problems receive attention, and so therapy begins—geared to the patient's needs and using the resources of the therapeutic team as required. Usually treatment commences by a period in the hospital, where group therapy is started, often on the day of admission, and continued throughout the hospitalization stay.

Treatment continues in an outpatient clinic nearest the patient's home and is also determined by the patient's needs and the needs of his family. The length of formal treatment varies but, in general, it is well to recognize that alcoholism is a *chronic* condition and requires not just months but often years of therapy. The family's needs are just as important as those of the alcoholic himself.

Goals of therapy for alcoholics are similar to those in other chronic illnesses: to avoid meddlesome manipulation and unwholesome intervention, to set attainable goals with the patient, and to help the patient to realize as fully as possible his own potentialities. It is not easy to say who make the best therapists for alcoholics, but in addition to sound professional qualifications, what seems most desirable is a discernment of the patient's value as a human being and a capacity for seeing realistically into the future to what he may become.

Much has been written about what is essentially wrong with alcoholics. Alcoholics are included in virtually all psychological categories and psychiatric diagnostic groups. One's impression as to what ails them depends to an extent upon what group of alcoholics one gets to know. No specific alcoholic personality type has been clearly differentiated. Nevertheless, new research does not entirely confirm the extreme view that alcohol addiction is simply a non-specific symptom of an unlimited variety of psychopathological processes—as it were, a kind of final common pathway into which funnel any number of diverse maladaptive sequences. There appears a pattern of character traits, including estrangement or separateness from people (even with a façade of outgoing, sociable behavior) dependency, depression, hostility, and immaturity, which varies from patient to patient. This character disorder has been seen as emerging from early deprivation and disturbance of the mother-child relationship. This basic disorder is not limited to alcoholics but is seen to be—along with cultural and probably physiological factors—as necessary in the cause of alcoholism.

New studies also suggest that alcoholics are more dependent upon (and probably more vulnerable to) their environment, so that engagement with the ongoing reality of present experience is especially difficult. This interface between the past and the future—this leading edge at which we must all confront life—may, for the alcoholic, become intolerable. For him the past may stalk him with its disappointments and guilt; the future may be a spectre of fearful anxiety; but the present is simply impossible.

There are several ways in which people try to cope with this problem of their engagement with the present (this *dyschronism,* as we might call it). It seems that some alcoholics—possibly all at some stage or other of their sickness—try to convert reality into some inner transcendent experience of their own choosing, abandoning the rough, hard, ordinary world of daily human give and take. Some people try to achieve this through narcotic drugs like morphine, and there are now newer "mind changing" chemicals through which one may have experiences "out of this world." Whether and to what extent such chemicals may have therapeutic uses is now being investigated.

For some alcoholics their drug of choice (alcohol) serves, like the barbiturates and other sleep-inducing sedatives, to obliterate consciousness altogether and simulate death. For others, alcohol addiction appears rather like addiction to food in which the threatened organism seeks to protect itself organically by unrestrained intake of nourishment. Finally, it sometimes appears that the alcoholic is like the work addict whose insatiable search for status and response to his unconscious needs drive him in a squirrel-cage of work activity quite unrelated to objective motivation. Actually, some inadequately treated alcoholics may stop drinking only to assume another of these addictive patterns—like work addiction with its possible sequelae of peptic ulcers or coronary disease.

It is infinitely worthwhile to study at first hand the alcoholic's sickness. This is a potent resource in research in causes, treatment, and prevention. Our approach ought always to be preventive; and early case-finding, diagnosis, treatment, and research are essential to the development of successful preventive measures. Alcoholism is an expression not only of individual disorder, but also of broad pathologies in society as a whole and calls for over-all study of, and concern for, problems of human ecology.

I have alluded to medical, psychological, and other modalities of treatment. The way of recovery for the alcoholic can be illuminated by general practitioners, social workers, nurses, psychiatrists, members of Alcoholics Anonymous (AA), and many others. Perhaps in closing, a word about religion is appropriate. AA is always demonstrating for all to see that alcoholics are getting well within a fellowship that accepts the need of God's help. The Church is a holy fellowship—a sacred community in which alcoholics and their families can find strength. Possibly for many an alcoholic there may be an answer to his existential problem in a sacramental view of life, that endows and invests each ordinary passing moment of present reality with grace and hence value. Possibly in the Church he may know God as an immanent, loving Being, who cares for man and comes to meet him and remains with him at every present moment everlastingly. Because God forever confronts and sustains man at the interface of the present, we may pray that "those things may please him which we do at this present." God being our present guide, "we may so pass through things temporal, that we finally lose not the things eternal."

THE
MENTALLY
DISTURBED

By SMILEY BLANTON

> Those who are unable to face life and are regarded as "mental cases" are "neighbors" to Smiley Blanton.

SMILEY BLANTON has had a life-long devotion to the study of mentally and emotionally disturbed people. Interested in drama, especially Shakespeare, he was on the stage for a time, his interest in character study leading him eventually into medicine and psychiatry.

After graduating from Vanderbilt University and taking graduate work at Harvard, Dr. Blanton received his M.D. from Cornell University College of Medicine in 1914. He then served as house physician at Phipps Psychiatric Institute, Johns Hopkins Hospital, and later at Queens Square Hospital for the Paralyzed and Epileptic in London.

In 1917 Dr. Blanton was psychiatrist for the City of New York, resigning to enter the Army where he served for a time as director of the Psychiatric Ward of Fort Slocum Hospital and as psychiatrist for the Second Division, Overseas Service.

Dr. Blanton was professor of Speech and Mental Hygiene for ten years at the University of Wisconsin, organizing and directing the Minneapolis Child Guidance Clinic; and assistant professor of Psychiatry at the University of Minnesota Medical School from 1924 to 1927. From 1933 to 1937 he was assistant professor of Psychiatry at Cornell University College of Medicine, and is associate professor emeritus of Clinical Psychiatry at Vanderbilt University College of Medicine. In 1929-30 Dr. Blanton worked with Dr. Sigmund Freud in Vienna, continuing this work in the summers of 1935 to 1938 in both Vienna and London.

A Diplomate of the American Board of Psychiatry and Neurology and of the Royal College of Physicians and Surgeons (in psychological medicine), Dr. Blanton is associate founder and director of the American Foundation of Religion and Psychiatry and director of the Religio-Psychiatric Clinic of the Marble Collegiate Church in New York.

In addition to writing many magazine and medical journal articles, Dr. Blanton is the author of *Love or Perish* and *Now or Never—The Promise of the Middle Years.*

The Mentally Disturbed

STUNNED fellow-workers stood about in the corridors of the office as the word spread. Yes, it was a nervous breakdown that had been causing the absence of a trusted fellow employee. For a while there was disbelief among the people who had known the person in one of the most intimate relationships our society affords—a working one—and then followed unbroken silence. There simply was nothing left to say, except to repeat the famous words of tiresome old Polonius of *Hamlet,* who, when reporting to the King and Queen about Hamlet, said:

> Your noble son is mad;
> Mad call I it; for, to define true madness,
> What is't but to be nothing else but mad?

Yet how foolish we are to think of insanity as old Polonius —that it is a strange, alien, unexplainable thing that befalls others, but never ourselves. How like the battle-weary soldier whose bravery stems from the fact that in his mind he repeats to himself, "Always they, but surely, Lord, never I."

Perhaps it would be pleasant to feel confident that it would in fact "always be they, but never we." But what a shallow Paradise we seek, for within themselves these very same "mad" people share life's heartaches and problems just as we all must do. The only difference between us is that they have broken under the strains their lives have forced upon them. Their minds have been unable to absorb the shocks of living, and they have withdrawn into a world of their own making.

There are many technical definitions for insanity, each drawn from the outward symptoms that each form forces upon the patient. Often the cause is obvious to even the most casual observer, but the cure in most cases remains the ability of the psychiatrist to make the person sincerely desire to return to the living.

No man can predict what or how much strain a person will break under, and it seems safe to say that this breaking point varies widely, depending in all probability upon the background of the person undergoing the strain. It has been my experience in investigating cases that patients break after having been under pressure for some period of time; that then some incident, large or small, pushes the balance scale and the patient regresses into his own fantasy world. The following actual case histories will best serve to illustrate my points.

My first encounter with Mrs. A came in a ward of one of the many fine mental hospitals provided by the State of New York. She was a thin, dark woman of about forty-five, not unattractive looking, yet on her face was a vague smile. Her outward appearance seemed to indicate that she did not mind being in the hospital and she laughed at one or two jokes I told her.

It wasn't long before she began to tell me of her twelve

children. Some had married, others were in high school or in the lower grades. She then told me, with a delightfully happy look on her face, that she would soon have still another child. When I asked how this could be when her body showed no signs of pregnancy, she merely smiled and said, "Yes, O yes, I *am* going to have another baby very soon."

As I searched through the past of my patient, I learned that the woman had come from one of the Middle East countries to marry a man of her own nationality whom she had never known before—she was in fact a sort of "picture bride." After eighteen years of married life, she had been unable to become pregnant, although she consulted doctors who assured her they could find no medical reason for her not becoming pregnant. Her husband's irritation, because she did not have a child, worsened and Mrs. A grew more and more distressed, feeling within herself that she was in some way failing in her duty to her husband. When her husband told her he was going to divorce her, she became agitated; finally her actions became noticeably abnormal, and she was confined to the psychiatric hospital.

It must be apparent that this woman wanted children so badly that her mind broke under the strain. When her husband asked for a divorce, it represented to her a situation more than she could stand and her unconscious took over. Mrs. A went to live in a world filled with her own dream children, where reality could no longer hurt her.

Mrs. A's condition was what we call dementia praecox or schizophrenia—the personality has split and the person completely rejects reality. What might seem to the untrained person a strange and puzzling situation, now becomes quite clear. Any woman who wishes for children and cannot have them might share Mrs. A's conflict, but she does not necessarily break under the strain. Whether Mrs. A broke because of physical weakness in her make-up or because she did not have the emotional, intellectual, and spiritual resources to meet the crisis of the divorce, on top of her disappointment because of her inability to have children, we do not know. Perhaps if she had known God as a forgiving and close friend, she might have shared her longings and found comfort.

The problem of disappointment at not having children is not a new one, but there are better ways to solve it than succumbing to self-pity and finally to complete withdrawal from life. It is a known fact that some of life's greatest troubles have been transformed into gifts of art that have weathered generations of time.

In 1775 Charles Lamb was born in London, a sickly child whose speech was marred by marked stuttering. When he was twenty-one years old his sister, in a fit of rage, murdered their mother by stabbing her to death. To Charles Lamb this act, coupled with his own afflictions, meant that mental weakness was an inherited family trait. Being a cripple and a stutterer kept him from being close to any woman, and he felt that he dared not have children lest they inherit some mental weakness. The desire for children never left him and it became part of his writings, where he found a substitute for his starved emotional life.

In the beautiful "Essays of Elia" there is one called "Dream Children: A Reverie." In this essay he speaks to his dream children, Alice and John, of their grandmother, who was a housekeeper in a great house in Norfolk, and of the wonderful holidays he spent there. At the close of the essay the soul of the first Alice, Charles Lamb's dream wife,

looked out at her eyes with such a reality of representment, that I became in doubt which of them stood there before me or whose that bright hair was; and while I stood gazing, both the children gradually grew fainter to my view, receding, and still receding till nothing at last but two mournful features were seen in the uttermost distance, which, without speech, strangely impressed upon me the effects of speech; 'We are not of Alice, nor of thee, nor are we children at all.'

Charles Lamb shared the same heartache as our Mrs. A, but he met it through an expression of the fantasy in his work and in so doing gave the world one of the most beautiful essays of the English tongue. It was this sharing of his troubled heart that kept him sane.

Frequently other people, often those who are closest to us, force us to make decisions that our minds refuse to accept as just. We hate them and guilt takes its heavy toll. Where no forgiveness can be found, our unconscious mind punishes us. The attempts of the human heart to master, without forgiveness, the resentment in the deeper mind may cause a mental breakdown. Such was the case of Mr. B, whom I met in a state mental hospital in a western state.

Mr. B was a tall, thin man who might have been described as quite distinguished looking, had it not been for the tears which streamed down his cheeks as he sat weeping. I spoke to him gently, asking, "What troubles you?" "I have lost my birthright," he said; "God has damned me to Hell." I asked him what this lost birthright was and he answered, "It's a little girl." "How old is she now?" I asked. "About eight," he said. I then asked him if he could see her and he said, "Oh yes, she is standing right there, dressed in a blue dress with a red ribbon around her hair. But I have lost my birthright and God has damned me to Hell." He shook with sobs.

Although there plainly was a similarity between the cases of Mrs. A and Mr. B, the latter's reaction to the situation was quite different. He not only felt that he had lost his birthright and would henceforth suffer eternal damnation, but he had bizarre hallucinations of actually seeing a child's image in front of him.

Reviewing the history of Mr. B, we learned that he had been an only child, subjected to over-protection from both his parents. The family owned a prosperous dairy farm, and when his father died while the boy was in his early teens, Mr. B and his mother continued to run the farm quite successfully. His mother was a very domineering woman whose over-attachment to her son was magnified when she lost her husband. She constantly maintained that she wanted her young son to find a wife, but always found fault with any girl he chose.

At the age of thirty, Mr. B met a nice girl in a neighboring town, who was quite suitable to become his wife. But again his mother interfered, complaining that the young woman was not nearly good enough for her son. His relationship with the woman continued, but by now the influence of his mother was too strong for him to rebel and to marry her as he wished to do. When the woman became pregnant as a result of their relationship, Mr. B wished even more to marry her. In fact he felt that they were secretly engaged and would marry soon. His mother, when she learned of the pregnancy, called the young woman immoral and unfit for her son. Once again he accepted his mother's decision and did not marry.

The child was born—a beautiful little girl—but under the circumstances the young woman could not rear the child and the baby was placed with an agency for adoption, and as is always the case, the details of the adoption were concealed from the mother.

Three years later Mr. B's mother died, and soon after he married the girl. They were unable to have any more children and before long Mr. B began to worry about his "lost" child. He began an endless search to find his baby, but of course his efforts were fruitless. After five years of marriage and longing for his child, his behavior became so strange, manifested in constant weeping and the claim that he'd lost his birthright, that his wife was forced to commit him to the State Hospital for the Insane. The little girl would have been about eight years of age when I spoke to him in the hospital.

I am sure that if any of us had a child adopted and knew we would never see the child again, we might very well find ourselves depressed and weeping in the lonely night. This in itself is a natural reaction to what could only be described as a tragic situation. The great majority of people, however, would somehow manage to take this shock without having a mental breakdown.

It should be noted, however, that with very few exceptions anyone will break if the pressure becomes great enough. For example, during the campaign with the Gauls, Julius Caesar captured the great King Vercingetorix, bringing him in chains to lead the procession of Caesar's "Triumph" in Rome. After the ceremony the brave King was put in an old abandoned well with several of his captured soldiers. The soldiers died, despite the fact that they were given food and water. After three months in such a situation, the brave King became quite mad.

We all have a primitive, childish side to our unconscious which finds its way to the surface when we are under pressure or in sleep. Each night when we fall asleep, our minds regress back to this primitive side in dreams. But as normal persons, we know that these are only dreams, for insight is the difference between the sane and the insane. You can have the strangest and most bizarre ideas and keep sane, if you recognize that they are abnormal. This realization is the crucial test.

Dream worlds are fun, and often children as well as adults indulge in them. I have known many children who had "dream" playmates they talked to and played with, but they did not actually believe that they were real children. I know of one little girl of seven who has had such a dream play-mate since the age of three. She has named her dream friend Carol, and has endowed her with the ability to do many things that she, herself, has been forbidden to do. She will inform her mother, "Carol has a two-wheeler." "Carol has a baby sister and a baby brother." She says, "Carol says it never rains in Florida"; and when her mother asks how Carol knows this, the little girl answers, "She used to live there." As the child grows older her dream playmate seems to be disappearing and is now used only to illustrate to her mother that other little girls have far greater privileges than she.

There are many types of schizophrenics, not all of which are found in mental hospitals. We have all encountered people who feel that others are persecuting them (Para-noia), and it is difficult to draw the line between those who have a real reason and those with a persecutory trend.

Some people who are hard of hearing often fancy that others are talking about them, or taking advantage of the disability to talk about them disparagingly. Yet quite often these deaf people will refuse to wear a hearing aid. The in-teresting thing is that inside of all of us there is a potential paranoia. Under the right set of circumstances we can all be made to feel persecuted, but only rarely to a degree that makes for mental illness.

There is another type of mental abnormality which is not as strange as schizophrenia, called manic-depression. This condition is characterized by alternating stages of depression and elation. The depressive stages are marked by: (1) sad-ness; (2) self-criticism; and (3) slowness in thinking and activity. Patients suffering from this mental illness often accuse themselves of numerous crimes and moral misde-meanors. One must be extremely careful—especially the minister or priest—lest they accept these confessions at their face value.

The manic-depressive while in the depressive stage may change suddenly—within a few hours—and become highly excited and over-active. This elated phase is characterized by: (1) elation; (2) over-activity; and (3) wild flight of ideas. For instance, the person might start to say one thing when immediately someone else takes his attention, and he jumps from one thought to another, never finishing anything. A typical conversation might range from: "There is a building outside in front of us. The cars are going down the street. Children have red hats on." The manic-depressive is unable to keep any logical train of thought. This is caused by inability to keep their attention fixed on one train of thought.

Another type of acute depression is called "symptomatic depression," which occurs as a direct result of some actual situation. The symptoms manifest themselves in many forms. For example, a person might become so depressed with the world situation as to sell his property at a time when selling is unnecessary. On the other hand the patient while in the manic state might start to buy things foolishly, or start in a business venture without giving it proper thought and preparation.

Not very long ago a man came to the American Foundation of Religion and Psychiatry for emotional guidance. It developed that he had once owned a highly prosperous dairy farm and a lucrative automobile agency. He gradually became so depressed at the conditions of the world that he convinced himself the world was doomed and that the United States would soon have an economic depression that would have everyone standing in bread lines. Despite the many friends who tried to persuade him not to sell his business, he did so. When he came to us, his depressive state had ruined him financially. Here was the case of a man who was sick, but not quite sick enough to be confined to a hospital, where he could have been prevented from hurting himself.

In another similar case a man who had been in the depressed stage suddenly shifted to the elated stage and felt that nothing he did could possibly fail. This man had a good job and his mind held a great many fruitful ideas. One of these was the forming of an exclusive employment agency to assist executives, customarily earning salaries of from ten thousand a year and up, to find positions. When he discussed his plans with us, we pointed out that although the idea sounded good, he had no previous experience in the field. He would not be dissuaded, however, and his arguments that such an agency was needed were quite rational. Against his wife's advice and our counsel, he went ahead with his plans for the agency, allowing no time to investigate the employment agency field. A suite of elaborate offices was rented and staffed with two secretaries, at a considerable cost. He lacked only two things, applicants and clients. His wife was in complete despair, and before two months had passed the man was committed to a psychiatric hospital. Unfortunately, during the two months he lost almost all of his money on a scheme that was doomed to failure from the beginning—another case where the extent of the illness was diagnosed too late to prevent the patient from injuring himself.

Everyone stores away a great deal of resentment, real and fancied, in the repository of his unconscious mind. It is natural to feel resentment toward loved ones, for they are responsible for the forced curbing of primitive drives and desires in their children. We have all felt at times that if it were not for a loved one, "we could do as we please." These thoughts are rejected by our conscious mind and pushed back into our subconscious which, strangely enough, punishes us for having this resentment toward those whom our conscious mind feels we should love. The subconscious conscience is often cruel and savage in its judgment of us. Often when a loved one dies, the grief over the loss produces a death-built association; for when we wish a loved one away, we are secretly wishing he were dead. The thought might be unconscious, but when that death does come, those very secret thoughts come forth to haunt us. The cruel unconscious conscience punishes us.

There are frequent examples of these exaggerated feelings of guilt in all of us. A case that came to our attention at the American Foundation of Religion and Psychiatry about a year ago concerned a woman who was deeply depressed and needed some sort of professional guidance to find her way back to a normal healthy existence. She had been grieving for three years over the death of her husband and was reluctant to do anything, to meet new friends or increase her social activity. Instead, she preferred to sit alone, depressed and friendless. Her husband had been a highly successful business man and they had been quite close. They had loved each other it seemed for a full and satisfying twenty-five years of married life, but also there had been considerable friction between them. Actually she had often felt a deep resentment toward him which she only dimly realized.

Her husband had suffered a coronary thrombosis but had been getting along quite well since the first attack, and it looked very much as though he would recover and live for some years. One evening he told her that he wasn't feeling very well and she suggested that perhaps it would be best if she telephoned the doctor. Her husband forbade her to call the physician, saying, "I just saw him today and I was all right. There is no sense in calling him now." She did not call, and her husband died in his sleep that very night.

When she came to us, she accused herself of being the cause of her husband's death. In her mind she rationalized that she had neglected him by not insisting that the doctor be called as she had wanted to, thereby causing his death. We pointed out that she could hardly have done so when he had made such a point of refusing to have her call the doctor, and besides, since her husband had undergone a complete physical examination just a few hours before, there would have been nothing more the doctor could do. In heart cases, it is not unusual for the heart to appear perfectly normal even just before an attack. An occlusion occurs in the arteries leading to the heart, taking only seconds, and death ensues. For such cases there can be no such thing as medical insurance, for it might happen in hours, months, or years—possibly never. No physician can be sure of the strength of the arteries involved.

Through our conversations we learned that this woman had resented her husband far more than she knew, feeling that he had been unfair, parsimonious, and selfish with her. Yet she had loved him, even though she also felt a great deal of hate toward him. When he died her superego told her, "You hated him and now you've killed him." True, he had frustrated her, and she did in her unconscious want to get rid of him at times. Deep in our unconscious minds we all have death wishes toward those who would dare to frustrate our "mighty and autocratic egos."

It required some months of psychotherapy, which included counseling with her minister, to make her religion more real to her, before our combined forces could remove the morbid guilt feeling she had developed. It was quite true that she had not done everything she should have done as a wife, but—as we pointed out—it was also true that he had not done all he should have as a husband. She had done the best she could, and there was no real reason for her to feel guilty. By showing her where she had succeeded during their twenty-five years together and how much happiness there had been, although perhaps there were times that were a little less than perfect, we guided her out of her depression and she again took a place in the world.

These pointless feelings of guilt are one of the most serious problems the religious teacher and the psychiatrist must deal with, for they are for the most part real only to the person experiencing them. Often the guilt leads to suicide, unless guidance can be given. One of our patients came to us so depressed that she informed me that she was actually contemplating taking her own life, but her religious training had thus far restrained her. She had become pregnant just before her husband was called into the army. They already had four children, and she had been in poor health. The family was not a wealthy one, indeed they were quite poor. Knowing she would be alone she felt that she could not go through another pregnancy, and she got rid of the unborn infant.

Religion had played an important part in the life of this woman, yet even after she asked God to forgive her, she continued to feel depressed and guilty. During our talks it became obvious that she had always pictured God as a cruel, punishing, unforgiving power, whose righteous wrath she was feeling as due punishment for her grievous sin. When the psychiatrist explained to her that she should not feel guilty but should, in her heart, feel the forgiveness she so sincerely sought, she replied, "How do you know? You are not a minister or a priest. I really am a guilty person."

It was only when the minister was able to give this woman a completely new concept of God—as a loving God who comes out to meet us as a father, as in the parable of the Prodigal Son—a God who is always ready to forgive us when we desire to lead a new life and sincerely ask to be forgiven for our mistakes of the past, that she was at last able to truly forgive herself. Her guilt and depression became a forgotten thing as she grew to know and understand God.

I need not stress here the many changes in behavior that occur as a result of disease or injury to the brain. Frankly, we know very little of the relationship of the brain to the mind. One great English neurologist once said of our knowledge, "The skull might as well be stuffed with cotton as far as we know of the relationship of the mind to the brain." About all we do know is that we must have a brain in order for the mind to function. We know that it is the front part of the brain that underlies our thinking. Yet we have also known great portions of this to be destroyed by injury or disease without seriously impairing mental capacity.

I would like to emphasize one curious thing which I observed repeatedly during my years of practice. Whatever injury is inflicted on the brain—arteriosclerosis lessening the blood supply to the brain or brain tumor or hemorrhage —the changes that follow in your mental life are governed to an extent by the fundamental deep-seated and deep-rooted personality you have developed for yourself.

One of the most common physical conditions of the mind is called senile dementia. The cause of this is arteriosclerosis of the arteries of the brain which in effect causes a partial closing off of the blood supply to the brain. The person begins to suffer from loss of memory, especially for recent events, the reasoning power becomes affected and he or she can no longer think clearly. Loved ones—even their own children—become strangers, as their minds slowly die. The condition is doubly tragic in that the people who once loved the person afflicted watch their loved one slip slowly into death of the mind while their healthy bodies live on. There are many degrees of the condition, reaching to the point where the patient becomes little more than a human vegetable—completely dependent upon others for food and attention to personal needs.

The medical reasons for senile dementia are comparatively easy to understand, but just what starts the condition defies answer. Age is, of course, the big factor, but perhaps once again the largest preventive known is the real desire for life. The condition itself is most dangerous and presents a serious situation when people who have positions of importance in business, politics, medicine, or any of a number of endeavors directly affecting the lives of others are involved. People in the early stages of senility may still hold positions where important decisions are required, yet they are incapable of making them. People so entrenched cannot be forced out without the consent they very often refuse to give. It has been my experience that few people actually become senile, no matter how great the arterial change, if they have always done constructive thinking and if they have faced the problems of life with courage and vigor.

There are many scientists who believe that all mental conditions are caused by some definite physical change in the brain or some chemical change in the body. There are even a few who believe that chemistry is the true answer to all ills of the mind. But they haven't looked nearly deep enough, nor does there seem to be other than the most superficial proof of this. Still the opinion is widely held.

My experience has taught me that schizophrenia and depressive psychoses are not caused by any physical or chemical changes in the body, but are rather the backwash of emotional responses channeled in the wrong directions. I firmly believe that we must look to each man's fundamental personality, his relationship with men and God. It is only through the study of these relationships and where they have failed that we can hope to understand the reasons why such things as mental breakdowns occur.

The prophets and poets have all realized the complexity of the human spirit. In 1600, the insane were thought to be possessed by the devil, for their simple reasoning told them that most certainly the insane were lacking in the quality that makes men like God—rationality. And so they assumed that God had deserted the insane and the devil had taken over.

The very essence of modern psychiatry and psychoanalysis was described generations ago by Shakespeare in *Macbeth*. When Lady Macbeth urges her husband to kill Duncan, his King, so that he may inherit the throne, she tells him:

> . . . I have given suck, and know
> How tender 'tis to love the babe that milks me;
> I would, while it was smiling in my face,
> Have pluck'd my nipple from his boneless gums,
> And dash't the brains out, had I so sworn as you
> Have done to this.

But as the play continues, Macbeth moves from one horrible deed to another, and poor Lady Macbeth's part in the murder of Duncan returns to haunt her until finally her mind breaks under the strain. As she wanders in a daze, she keeps repeating:

Here's the smell of blood still; all the perfumes of Arabia will not sweeten this little hand; Oh, Oh, Oh!

After listening to this repetitious refrain, her physician says:

> Foul whisperings are abroad; unnatural deeds
> Do breed unnatural troubles; infected minds
> To their deaf pillows will discharge their secrets.

> More needs she the divine than the physician—
> God, God forgive us all! . . .

It is profound mystery how a great artist, even William Shakespeare, could have ideas about insanity and its treatment which are as modern as can be found in any hospital in the world today.

At the time when it was thought that the devil and witches were the cause of insanity and that people had to be treated cruelly in order to drive the devil out, Shakespeare has Macbeth say these words to the doctor about his mentally sick wife which is the most modern prescription for psychotherapy that we have today:

> Canst thou not minister to a mind diseased;
> Pluck from the memory a rooted sorrow;
> Raze out the written troubles of the brain;
> And with some sweet-oblivious antidote
> Cleanse the stuff'd bosom of that perilous stuff
> Which weighs upon the heart?

THE LEGALLY UNDER-PRIVILEGED

By JOHN S. BRADWAY

Those unable to protect themselves legally in times of adversity, financially helpless in face of the law, are "neighbors" to John Bradway.

JOHN SAEGER BRADWAY has been perhaps the most active leader in the legal aid clinic movement for many years. After receiving his A.B. and A.M. from Haverford College, he studied law at the University of Pennsylvania and was admitted to the Pennsylvania Bar in 1914. He entered private practice in Philadelphia and served as assistant attorney of the Philadelphia Legal Aid Society until 1920, when he became chief counsel of the Philadelphia Municipal Legal Aid Bureau.

Mr. Bradway was secretary of the National Association of Legal Aid Organizations, a post which he held from 1922 until 1940 when he became president for a two-year period. In 1929 Mr. Bradway became professor of Law and director of the Legal Aid Clinic at the University of Southern California, and from 1931 until he recently retired, was professor of Law at Duke University and director of the Legal Aid Clinic there, also serving as visiting professor at the University of North Carolina School of Social Work.

Professor Bradway is a member of the North Carolina State Conference of Social Service of which he was President in 1940-41; the National Conference of Social Work; the National Association of Social Workers; the North Carolina Mental Hygiene Association; and the North Carolina State Probation Committee. He is also a member of the American Bar Association and the Bar Associations of California, Pennsylvania, and North Carolina and has served as chairman of their Legal Aid committees.

Professor Bradway, author of legal books and contributor to law reviews, was honored by Haverford College with an LL.D. in 1957.

The Legally Underprivileged

*T*HE BASIC facts of professional life were not born in my infant consciousness. Nor did they burst upon me in some instant of dazzling inspiration. Rather they made themselves apparent in a series of dimly experienced stages, during and after law school, as I groped in an effort to understand them.

The first fact to force itself upon my bemused perception was that in the United States there were great numbers of people in the lower income brackets who, because they had little or no money in their pockets, had difficulty in obtaining certain public or quasi-public commodities that are within easy reach of those in better financial circumstances. Next came the revelation that one of these commodities was justice-according-to-law. It took me some time to realize that the guarantee in the Constitution of "equal protection of the law" was not self-executing and that the words were no more magical than any other words until somebody came along to give them life. Of course, that somebody had to be a lawyer since it was against the law for anyone else to practice this profession. Later all these discoveries of mine receded into a state of secondary importance, and the most amazing stage in my self-education came when I acknowledged that I, individually and professionally, had a personal responsibility to do something about bringing together justice and the poor.

It was not easy to make the transition from intellectual to emotional thinking. I could with considerable equanimity "know" poverty and its consequences in an objective, impersonal manner. Other people's problems I could bear with an easy mind. They were what one reads about in books or is told about by authority. But when I developed the ability to think emotionally and subjectively, when I came to see that perhaps the most important aspect of the professional life was not the problem but the person who had the problem, when I experienced contact with such a person firsthand, the world became a much more troublesome place. Now the baby had been laid directly on my doorstep. I had opened the door and had seen it lying there. I could no longer shut the door; but what else could I, should I, was I going to do?

The first crack in my smugness, the first step in my emotional growth, the initial firsthand contact I had with a person in need of legal help but financially unable to attain it, came during my third year in law school. One winter evening I was studying at my desk in the law library—a large place and, at that hour, dark and deserted—the door opened, and in stepped not another student as I had expected, but a neat little old lady who made her way to my desk and asked me if I would advise her. I graciously indicated that even an Olympian like myself was willing to be questioned. Inwardly, however, I was stunned, for I was actually talking to a real client. Not once, in the three years of my novitiate, had I been confronted with any real clients. Legal problems of X, Y, and Z had been presented to us daily by amiable, keen scholarly gentlemen who directed our attention to cases appearing on the printed page and to the class discussion—a procedure that had prepared me to be only an observer. But here, with no effort on my part, I suddenly found myself in the unfamiliar role of participant. This was the real thing. My formal training up to this point was merely a sort of shadow boxing—necessary, of course, but oversimplified by reason of the omission of the human equation. My thinking now became distinctly emotional, and nobody had ever taught me how to do that kind of thinking.

The lady told me her story. She wanted protection from a landlord who, it appeared, was a very unreasonable individual. But I had never taken a course in Landlord and Tenant law and could not even think, under the impact of this startling personage, how to begin looking up a point of law in an unfamiliar field. Realizing that I was a broken reed, the old lady thanked me politely for my time and, still resolute, made her way off into the darkness. Immediately a wave of humiliation at my own obvious incompetence swept over me. I tried to rationalize the experience but could find no basis for comfort, and for some weeks I was crushed. Yet this old lady was of the greatest help to me in that she had forced me to realize that there were poor people—probably many—who had legal problems and did not know how to get them solved.

The next step in my enlightenment came when the Board of Bar Examiners granted me my license, and a law firm accepted me as sort of glorified office boy. The first day I reported for practice, one of the members of the firm told me that he had recently been appointed chief attorney for the local Legal Aid Society and he inquired whether I would be interested in spending some time in legal aid work. Although I had no idea what a legal aid society might be, I assented; and that afternoon my chief and I wended our way to a less expensive section of the city, to a small office in an unpretentious office building. There, in the waiting room, were some forty people obviously in the lower economic brackets and clearly people with problems. In the rear office were two tables and a desk. My chief took his place at one table, I sat at the other, and the secretary— a marvel of competence, as I came to learn—sat between us. Without ado the secretary ushered in two clients. One of them composed himself at the table of my chief; the other came to me. Here, indeed, was my first *real* client, but I was no better prepared to talk to him than I had been a few months before to the old lady. However, I was now a member of the bar and had some obligations.

During the long afternoon, I wrestled with this one client and his really simple problem. My chief, with what seemed to me miraculous expedition and competence, disposed of the legal queries of the other 39 visitors, while I remained true to my one and only. Finally, about five o'clock, I dismissed my client and staggered out into the street to take a new look at the life into which I had been introduced. Two features of that look still remain clear in my mind. While I had a license, I felt that I lacked competence for the practice of law in any form. But even so, the legal vocation still had for me attraction and excitement, and my earnest hope was that someday I, too, might possess a professional manner, poise, and the ability to deal with the unexpected. This was the second step in my process of self-education.

Again time moved on. I am not sure whether the quality of my advice to members of the public improved; but I did manage to pick up some speed in dealing with their legal affairs. There were many clients, and they kept rolling in,

day after day, in an endless flood. Eventually I was ready
for still another step forward.

The occasion was a conference of people from all over the
country who were interested in legal aid work. In those
days there were not too many of them, but what fascinated
me was that the work, which I had until that time regarded
as purely local, was really national. Those attending the
conference were what we may call second-generation legal
aiders. In the first generation were people like the late
Arthur V. Briesen of New York, Rudolph Matz of Chicago,
and M. W. Acheson, Jr., of Pittsburgh, who had called the
first national legal aid conference in 1911. Acheson was
still active and full of ideas. In the second generation were
people like Reginald Heber Smith of Boston, who had just
published his book *Justice and the Poor,* which told the
whole story of legal aid up to that time, Leonard McGee of
New York, Forrest C. Donnell of St. Louis, Joel D. Hunter
of Chicago, to mention only a few. This second generation
group were all present at the national conference, and I had
a chance to meet them face to face.

They were the first pioneers of any sort with whom I had
ever had direct contact. They made me realize that something had to be done about the needs of legal aid clients,
and that a great deal was actually being done. To my lasting
satisfaction I received from these giants in the earth an invitation to serve as secretary of the newly formed National
Association of Legal Aid Societies. The chief problem of
this new organization was one of quantity—the need for
more local organizations.

At once I plunged into my new field of activity. Whereas
previously I had been in the front-line trenches; now I was
back at headquarters. Where formerly I had been meeting
clients; now I was constantly meeting with civic-minded
people who might be persuaded to sponsor or develop a

legal aid organization in their own community. Instead of telling impecunious individuals how to protect themselves from a variety of injustices—threatened, real, or imaginary —I was writing letters, reports, surveys. I made talks—or rather I made the same talk many times (and eventually it improved somewhat in quality). Through it all I noticed in myself a retreat from self-interest and a steadily increasing emphasis on idealism. The cause was more important than the proponents. It meant much to me to know first hand that everywhere I went there were people who were more concerned about what they could give their communities than what they might expect to get in return.

The national legal aid movement did not immediately sweep the country off its feet. Objectors rose in clouds. Probably what bothered most of them was that they did not understand very clearly what we were about. Consequently it seemed to them sound policy to oppose an organization on general principles. Their vocal protests fell into various well-defined categories. For example, some of them maintained that there was no need for organized legal aid work because unorganized work of this sort was done as a matter of course in every law office. Others suspected that under our suave exterior there lurked a subtle plan to promote socialized law. At the time socialized medicine was becoming highly controversial, and some observers in law did not like the looks of things. Still others prophesied that the immediate result in a community which set up a legal aid society would be a horde of applicants none of whom qualified in an economic sense for the service and many of whom would be the chronic malcontents and noisy troublemakers.

Eventually we found the answers to all these objections. We were able to convince some persons that it was not the lawyer but the client who created the need for organized legal aid; that too often clients did not know that there were lawyers prepared to render assistance without charge; and that even when they did know that there were such lawyers, they hesitated to sit down in the same law office waiting room alongside clients who were paying fees. To another group we replied that organized legal aid work, far from being the precursor of socialized law, was the best answer to the "menace." We even predicted that if legal aid was neglected, socialized law sooner or later was pretty certain to arrive. On one point the objectors were right. The creation of a law office especially dedicated to solving the problems of poor persons did raise a crowd of clients. But we soon discovered that the overwhelming majority of these people were bona fide clients entitled to the service. Those applicants who could pay a fee or were chronic complainers could readily be screened out. The remainder had meritorious legal claims but not much money in their pockets.

As I recall this period, I can see myself standing on platforms talking to audiences, answering questions, pleading for the hearers to accept our interpretation of the facts. Some of the responses were interesting. One morning following such a talk, an objector met me and said: "Last night you spoke quite fairly to us. But by God, if you were lying, we'll get you if it is the last thing we ever do." On another occasion when I had told my audience a story I regarded as not only amusing but relevant, a lady came up to me at the end of the meeting and said, "This is a serious occasion. Somebody should have told you." Then without another word, she turned and walked away. Obviously, I had not been serious enough.

After some twenty years, the vehemence of the objectors ebbed a bit. In some areas their voices even died away, and we began to hope that we had made our point; that the program we supported was in effect respectable. Thereafter the main promotional obstacle was local inertia.

Now it was time for me to take another step forward on the road to firsthand self-education. The focus of national legal aid attention shifted from the idea of quantity—a legal aid society in every town—to include a concept of quality. The word "equal" in the phrase "equal protection of the law," means equal in quality. The legal aid client deserves the rating of a first-class citizen. The fact that he cannot afford to pay for a commodity as basic as justice-according-to-law is no reason why we should expect him to be content with anything less than the quality of service dispensed by the leading local law offices.

The opportunity for me to introduce this concept of quality came when Justin Miller, then dean of the Law School at the University of Southern California, invited me to see what could be done about the problem of giving the law student practical training before his admission to the bar. The difficulty was one of long standing in the history of legal education. The traditional answer to it had been the law office apprenticeship. But in recent years, despite brilliant exceptions, a system which depended upon the law office as an educational center was being questioned seriously by those who had the future of the legal profession and the community at heart. We were not looking for a substitute for apprenticeship because that would suggest something of more or less secondary value to be used as a temporary replacement. Our search was for some device, some process, some concept, whereby the sort of work previously done by the law office in the educational field might be done even better.

We picked as the name of our remedy "legal aid clinic." The name "clinic" was used to suggest an analogy with the

work being done in the medical field. "Legal aid" indicated
the client group. There were already several legal aid clinics
in operation in connection with various law schools. But
they were generally cooperative ventures of the law school
and the local legal aid society. Our law school proposed to
assume full responsibility. The clinic was to move right in
under the roof of the law school—like the medical outpatient department in a teaching hospital.

As matters worked out, there were three elements in the
program to be promoted from the one office. Since in Los
Angeles there was no existing local legal aid service in
operation, we would supply it. This aspect of the program
we referred to as humanitarian. To be sure, law students
participated in the work under supervision. But as far as the
client was concerned, he received the equal protection of
the law as nearly as we could give it to him.

The second part of the program was definitely promotional. On leaving law school and engaging in law practice
in their home towns or elsewhere, the students would not
forget the firsthand contact they had with organized legal
aid work. They would see no reason to be afraid of it and
would generally agree that it fulfilled a distinct need in any
community. Therefore, they should become ambassadors,
proponents for the idea. This form of low-pressure promo-
tion might be somewhat slower than one bottomed on a staff
of paid advocates; but it had its own merits. Legal aid work
in most areas is, as someone has said, "the lengthened
shadow of some great man." We are sending out into the
profession a group of potential great men with shadows
ready to be lengthened in this direction. Furthermore, the
program was inexpensive and would give the resulting
movement a "grass roots" character, and not be something
imposed on a community from without.

The third aspect of the program was definitely educational. It was designed to provide the student with the most practical sort of training. On it we expended the major portion of our time and effort. Eventually we came upon a formula which seemed to provide a convenient point of departure. It was like this: if the object of legal education is to teach the student to think like a lawyer, the objective of the legal aid clinic was to train him to think like a general practitioner. One outstanding characteristic of the general practitioner is his ability to deal with the unexpected. The specialist knows pretty much what to look forward to when the door of his law office opens. But the general practitioner must be perpetually ready for anything.

At this stage I found myself retracing some of my early experiences. There was a repetition of the process of trial and error. Only now I was in the observer's seat. My task was to guide the student while he was going through the trial, tactfully point out the error, and suggest ways in which to avoid its recurrence.

When a client appeared I did not leave the student alone with him in the pious hope that the better man might win. I sat right there. Naturally the student errors I saw most clearly were the ones I myself had committed in what seemed like an earlier incarnation. If the student asked the wrong question, I had to resist the temptation of assuming a holier-than-thou attitude from which he might infer that he must have a mentality no higher than that of a moron. If he produced for my approval a draft of a letter with a sentence in which he had inadvertently dispensed with the customary verb, I was in a position to bring his humiliation home to him.

The problem of setting up a law school legal aid clinic in a city the size of Los Angeles was not too difficult. We devoted two years to the initial phases of our work with, I must hasten to add, the aid and comfort of a staff of remarkable and dedicated people. The continuance of the program in that city is due to their enthusiasm, foresight, and endurance. My own steps led me to Duke University in Durham, North Carolina, then a city of some "50,000, counting Republicans."

In this smaller center, opposition to the legal aid program developed from various quarters, some of it very vigorous. But there were other groups which welcomed us as a new and useful form of community service. In particular, our relations with the state and county welfare departments was heartening. In time the clamor of the objections quieted down, and we were free to switch our main attention to the development of a system of practical training for young lawyers.

Various possible illustrations of this phase of my development come to mind. Selection of one as typical is impossible because they covered so wide a range. The following, however, will give at least a glimpse. The reader is asked to imagine the scene: a student sits with me as we interview the client.

The client is a man about fifty years of age. He announces that he would like us to supply him with some legal authorities. It appears that he had been a party to litigation in another part of the state and in the trial court had lost. He is convinced that justice is on his side and that the Supreme Court will see matters his way. All he wants from us are the legal authorities. We inquire as to the lawyer representing him. He assures us that he does not have too high a regard for lawyers; that he is unrepresented; and that he intends to argue the case himself. We urge that the orthodox way to present a case to a court, especially an appellate court, is with the aid of counsel. He perseveres in his position. In other respects he was a legal aid client. We finally decide to humor him. We procure some relevant authorities which will speak on his side. He thanks us and departs in the general direction of the state capital. Both the student and I agree that this client is following a most unwise course.

A week later the client returns. This time he tells us he is on his way home. We express appropriate regret that he has lost the case and restrain from making the obvious "I told you so" comment. He replies: "Oh, you don't understand. I won."

To me it appeared that we were witnessing a very excellent illustration of the principle that it takes an exception to prove the rule. What the student really thought of the situation I never knew. I hope he was shocked. He might well have concluded that a professional man, necessarily a specialist, is wise never to underestimate the power of a layman.

The Legal Aid Clinic program also had its share of rough weather. The objectors were vigorous. They did not go so far as to argue that practical training was unnecessary for a lawyer. Rather their point was that it was not the proper function of the law school to provide it. The law office was the place. Our position was that any rigid allocation of function could hardly be justified even while the law office apprenticeship system was in effective operation. That system, however, was being subjected to increasing criticism, and we felt warranted in looking forward to the jurisdiction of the law school of tomorrow rather than to that of yesterday.

We could not avoid wondering what the criticism might reveal of the nature of the critic himself. Thus, one man might argue that the clinic was too expensive; that in comparison with a casebook course the cost per student and otherwise was fantastic. Our reaction was that whether a particular program was, or was not, too expensive depends not on the amount of the money spent but upon what one

received in return. We noted that other educational devices
—medical clinics, science laboratories, even the law library
itself—cost a lot more than a legal aid clinic, so that the
amount of money to be paid out was not necessarily the
stumbling block. We wondered if there might not be an
understandable reluctance on the part of some to go out
into the open market and raise money for a novelty. We
felt some confidence that the public would be willing to
pay for better-trained young general practitioners.

Another objector based his argument on the amount of
student time consumed. He would insist that with only three
years to devote to the educational process the student
should be fed on more "important" fare. We did not con-
cede that three years, or any other arbitrary period of time,
represented the limits of a proper legal education, even of
law school responsibility. To us it seemed that a procrustean
policy certainly had no place under modern conditions
where the body of law was expanding and developing year
by year. We thought the legal profession should be making
some effort to keep pace with the increased demands which
the public seemed to be making for wider professional
competence. Neither did we agree with the appropriateness
of the word "important." To us "important" had a subjective
content. Course A might seem important to one instructor;
Course B to another. Looking at the matter objectively, we
felt that we could give the law student enough practical
training in our course so that he would be anywhere from
two to five years ahead of the man who had not had that
benefit. We thought that period of time was worth saving.
It appeared to us that legal education was necessarily a life-
long task and that the law school might properly be available to the student not merely at the beginning but all the
way.

Finally, there were those critics who insisted that our

function was to teach the students how to fold a piece of paper. Such a critic was certainly not well-informed. We wondered about his willingness to comment without taking the trouble to get his facts before him, although from time to time we did come across students who did not know how to attend to basic details like folding a piece of paper, and we had to show him how. We did not, however, regard that as evidence that the clinic course was superficial. On the contrary, we valued our labors in the field of details as among the most important performed in any course in law school. We did not understand how a man could come all the way up the educational ladder through school, college, and two years of law school, and still have these blank spots in his training. Their existence was somebody's fault. We did not stop to inquire where the responsibility lay. What worried us was that if, with full knowledge, we permitted a man to go out into the world with the Duke label on him and to make mistakes of this sort, his reputation and the reputation of the school would certainly, and properly, suffer.

We saw our overall task in terms of three examinations which a law student must pass: the first, that given by the law professor; the second, that by the Board of Bar Examiners; and the third, that by the general public. We assumed that our obligations ran in favor of helping him through all three of these, but especially the last.

It is interesting to attempt to forecast the future of legal aid clinic work. There are promising signs. Some years ago, Charles H. Miller, Jr., went from North Carolina over the mountains to Tennessee and, at the University of Tennessee, set up a clinic quite similar to the one he and I had been operating at Duke University. Various law schools in larger centers have developed their contacts with the local legal aid society so that the students may learn not merely law but people and facts and law, all at the same time. It would seem that the clinic movement represents a development in the field of law which may be compared with that in psychosomatic medicine.

Here, as in all autobiographical papers, the story breaks off. It is unfortunate to feel that one must close the account before the journey comes to the end. But there are certain observations which, even now, are worth making.

There are poor people, many poor people, in this country. I have met all too many of them. They have problems, some of which require for solution the resources of the field of law. The orthodox machinery of the law and the legal profession was inadequate to deal with these problems in such a manner as to give the profession the public respect which its services deserve. Therefore, something had to be done. Somebody had to take action. It is a satisfaction to report that many people have taken that action, that something is being done. It is even more gratifying personally to remember that I have had a part in this process, perhaps a small part, but at all events not that of a spectator. If the movements already established continue with reasonable effectiveness for another generation, we may expect with some confidence that there will be few people who, because of their poverty, will be denied equal justice under law. We may still have a long way to go on our journey, but we have also come a respectable distance. What this means in a democracy is a matter for anyone's evaluation. My own reaction is to place a very high value upon it.

THE AGED
AND RETIRED

By ETHEL PERCY ANDRUS

Those retired, the aged, who feel no
longer needed by the society around
them, their tasks finished, are "neighbors" to Ethel Andrus.

ETHEL PERCY ANDRUS has worked for many years in furthering the status of retired teachers and, more recently, of all retired persons. After receiving her Ph.B. at the University of Chicago in 1903, she began a teaching career, becoming principal of Lincoln High School, Los Angeles, in 1916, where she developed an outstanding program of inter-ethnic understanding and individual development among the 2,500 pupils in an ethnically-mixed and deteriorating community. She held this post until her voluntary retirement in 1944, and during this period earned a B.S. from Lewis Institute and her A.M. and Ph.D. from the University of Southern California.

Always active in many education and community organizations, Dr. Andrus, since 1947, has been president of the National Retired Teachers Association which initiated, in 1956, the first policy of national scope to provide group hospital and surgical benefits to retired persons and established in 1954 at Ojai, California, the first retirement residence for teachers, of which she is director. She is also editor of the NRTA *Journal,* a quarterly mailed to some 60,000 members. Since 1958 Dr. Andrus has been president of the American Association of Retired Persons and editor of its magazine, *Modern Maturity.*

Among awards received by Dr. Andrus are: selection as National Teacher of the Year by the National Congress of Parents and Teachers and the National Education Association in 1954; awards for Service to Community and Youth in 1954 by the City of Glendale, the City and County of Los Angeles, and the State of California; Alumni Citation for Public Service, University of Chicago in 1955. Her own busy life is an example of the fruitful use of retirement years which is the thesis of Dr. Andrus' essay.

The Aged and Retired

"Old age, like every other ordinance of nature, ought not to be looked upon as evil. If people fancy that it will never come upon them and consequently complain of being taken by surprise, they have only themselves to thank for the delusion."—Cicero, *De Senectute*

"Grow old along with me! . . .
Our times are in his hand
Who saith, 'A whole I planned,
Youth shows but half; trust God: see all,
    nor be afraid!'—Robert Browning

*W*HEN we think about aging, the questions at once arise, When is a person aged? how old is old? But individuals, on the evidence of different cases, give different answers to these questions, so that we are forced further to ask, Is aging then, a relative term, or should we accept the arbitrarily fixed age of enforced retirement, 65 years, as the beginning of aging? Then, another question looms, Is aging desirable?

121

Aging has always been with us, but today aging is in the process of revolution. Science has lengthened our lives but science, through industry, has taken from us, in part, the means to enjoy that life in action. The stereotype of old age as a disease, increasingly costly and troublesome, however, is contradicted by the host of happy and productive oldsters participating and serving beyond the call of duty.

Retirement and aging have innumerable facets. A gracious physician gave me my first close-up view when he said to me, "Your father is suffering from atrophy of the optic nerve. Just how soon he will be blind, I can't say; but I suggest that you plan for his care and happiness with the knowledge that the disease is a progressive one." It was then I realized the possible bleakness of enforced and unexpected retirement.

The challenge to do something about it was, of course, an impelling one. Not only did I desire to help my father maintain for himself a meaningful future, but I sought to help forestall similar unforeseen tragedy in others. Feeling that selection and the pursuit of a hobby could be a mighty anchor to the windward, I installed in the high school of which I was then principal an avocational hour. Imagine my chagrin to find only cynical indifference and intolerant apathy toward this project. The expectancy of a need of play in one's life pattern apparently seemed senseless to most people. For a year the avocational hour struggled for life and acceptance, then died unwanted, mourned only by myself.

Not long afterward, as the lone woman member of our high school principals' group, I was made responsible for the organization's welfare program. I knew it only as a humanitarian operation and wondered just what might be my contribution to it.

I had not long to wait. One rainy Saturday a telephone

call came from a kindly shopkeeper in a town thirty miles away, summoning me to the assistance of an old woman who had once been a teacher. It was cold and drizzly when I arrived at the chicken house in which this woman lived. I knocked on the sagging door of that windowless shed, and assured the answering voice that I had come to say "howdy"—one teacher to another; and I asked if I might come in. Stockily built, with short grey hair, in an old coat much the worse for both age and wear, a woman withered of skin, with sunken cheeks but with the bluest and merriest of eyes, looked me over, smiling and putting me at my ease. "Just a friendly visit," I said; and I told her my name. Curiously enough, she knew it and, more curiously, I recognized hers and recalled her reputation as a Spanish teacher of some distinction.

When I asked if we might chat under cover out of the drizzle, she waved me to my car, and there she told me her story. Thriftily she had saved money enough to buy on installments some scenic acreage in Montrose, a charming section above Glendale, which she planned to subdivide. And so, accepting her $40-a-month teacher-retirement, she started out on her second career. But alas, the depression took away all opportunity for sale, and a devastating flood washed away the approaches to the property. Her high hopes were dashed. This little lady, who had been thrilled and moved on retirement by the tokens of appreciation she received, found herself, in the idle days that followed, lonely, unneeded, and forsaken. She lost her property. She had only her $40-a-month to live on, and had to make do with that. She dropped from her friends' sight and memory.

Against her expressed opposition our principal's organization outfitted her with glasses and dentures and gave her some financial aid. My next visit to a needy retired teacher showed me an equally depressing picture of retirement. Yet, in each instance, the woman had been outstanding in her profession and known as a dedicated teacher.

In my new assignment I saw ex-teachers forced, by the $60 teacher retirement salary of 1947, to lower their standards of living—they were pitiful both in their pride and in their need. Always having served as best they might, readily accepting what was accorded them, these teacher friends of mine needed self-assurance in order to state their case, not as they pictured, to a calloused lot of legislators, but to an informed public who would be glad and ready to respond.

All my contacts, however, were not folks in need. Often I saw about me men and women who, upon retirement, seemed to grow in spirit and in grace. I saw volunteer groups of these oldsters man community and church posts, serve as aides and counselors, as unpaid workers in the thousand-and-one jobs of neighborly or community concern. I saw men and women happily enrolled in the adult school of their neighborhood, working away at hobbies in the senior centers, holding half-time jobs—happy, normal, busy folk: needed, serving, growing old graciously.

My own learning process in this field of the aging increased when my mother—she who had brought light and color to my father's failing sight, who had created for him warmth and tenderness—fell seriously ill in her 90's. I retired immediately and devoted myself to her. Some time later, when again her old self, she said to me quite seriously, "I have been thinking a great deal lately about old age. Old age, Ethel, needs care as youth needs care, but it needs something more. It needs the desire to live, to continue planning and striving hopefully, to keep working at something worth-while, and then when at last old age becomes dependent, it needs someone to still care, or if there is no one to care, there should be community care which can make it easy to help those who now cannot help themselves to keep their dignity and their self-respect." I listened and wondered what I really knew about aging.

From my father I had learned that one can see beauty even in darkness. In so doing one can meet an impending disaster. Even in the normal process of aging, as my mother suggested, security and comfort need preparation with imaginative care.

From my friend in the chicken shed I had learned that the inner strength with which she met hardship can make even penury bearable, that there may be great wealth of spirit with little in one's purse. Even though we judged her case "pitiful," she did not feel a victim. Every day to her was a new triumph of wit and will.

I had learned from another friend who felt withdrawn and futureless the needless tragedy of building an image of herself as a person not needed. I learned too from my group of retired teacher friends, who suffered needless hardship without protest, the need of a sheltering group which could ask impersonally and righteously for what the individual might be embarrassed to ask for himself.

I learned, too, from those who had found fulfillment the comfort of companionship, the urgency to help where help is indicated, the conviction that life holds a challenge, and the obligation of each of us to make his family and his community a bit better and happier unit because of his life and living. I learned, too, the futility and the destructiveness of self-pity.

While aging is universal, it is really still intensely personal. Although the aged group is interesting statistically—often dramatically—it is not a homogeneous entity. In it we find great extremes: economically from vast wealth to utter penury, physically and mentally from the sprightly well-adjusted octogenarian to the senile chronic invalid with varying degrees of normalcy. Aged people are more than statistical material.

There are those who even in youth and adulthood have always felt abused and unprized. There are those who are chronically aggressive and pugnacious toward life and living. These, we can predict, will not enjoy a happily adjusted old-age. But to those others—the mature, the naturally passive, and the independent—older life can be pleasant and rewarding. And among them all is the common denominator of mutual needs and positive requirements.

Perhaps the most compelling drive is the wish to live. Progress in medicine has extended the span of man's lifetime by postponing death. And yet there is a hidden danger here. Dr. Davidson of New Jersey tells of a venerable and celebrated physician's saying, upon accepting an accolade from the younger members of his profession, "When one has escaped the lesser hazards of life—which is dying too young—he faces the greater hazard of living too long." A Chinese doctor asked what the speaker meant. How could living too long be a hazard? In his country the old man and the old woman are respected and given an important place in the community. Dr. Davidson did not know the answer, but reported that on the staff of the Essex County Hospital in New Jersey there are doctors from the four corners of the world and they testify that in their respective countries old people represent only 10 to 15 per cent of the mental hospital population and not 55 per cent as in the United States. Yet we comfort ourselves with Browning's plea, "Grow old along with me!"

Second only to the desire to live is the natural yearning to be wanted and needed, to feel that one's contribution to life is still essential. But this yearning challenges the oldster and impels him to give generously of himself, to circulate among his fellows, to participate actively in the little world about him, and to share whatever he may have of talent, strength, means, wisdom, or skill. This is the basis of his self-respect; in this way he earns his sense of dignity and worth.

Aging need not be synonymous with loneliness. No oldster need be without friends, if he himself seeks to be one; no one will be unsought if he is known to be kindly and ready to serve. There is no exercise better than reaching down and lifting another up, and no surer cure of loneliness.

Wilfred Funk, it is reported, in naming words that are vitally significant, listed these: the most bitter—*alone;* the saddest—*forgotten;* and the most tragic—*forsaken.*

Florence Nightingale at 31 felt that death alone could solve her distress, and Abraham Lincoln, we know, was a man of sorrow. But they both found their peace in caring for their fellow men. Only so do the elderly find solace in themselves, feeling grace working, faith replacing doubt, health overcoming sickness, and darkness giving way to light. This pronouncement may sound sentimental, but the medical profession assures us that it combines the finest of therapy with the soundness of common sense.

Longevity and health are not inherent rights; these privileges carry an obligation to earn them. The oldster must stop thinking of the treatment of his ills as merely applying a temporary patch to a worn fabric. He must think positively how to keep that fabric in shape for long and comfortable use. He need not put up with handicaps and infirmities that can be corrected. It must be admitted, however, that all of us have two-way feelings. We want to be independent, yet we want to be taken care of. We seek the reassurance of our earlier satisfying experiences when some one did take care of us. So often the aged, seeking affection and the assurance of being cared for and being important to someone, enjoy and prolong their disabilities. But their real need is to accept the disabilities of age and to live with them, adapting themselves to their physical limitations.

The elderly are often worried about money. Economic independence, in part, colors all the rest. The retired person is probably faced with having less income. Does this lesser income necessitate a change of residence? a lower standard of living? Retirement may cause no disturbance in the case of those who can earn a supplemental salary, but to the great majority the problem needs an honest facing. If income is smaller, is need of material things correspondingly less compelling? Smaller quarters and simplified housekeeping are found to be sensible *musts* with many oldsters. Health and accident insurance pay rich dividends in peace of mind. If social role and status are still a matter of pride and one's own personal concept of self remains undisturbed, changes in economic status and mode of living are accepted as matters-of-course by friends for whom, later perhaps, the same fate will be in store. For the truth is that wealth and freedom from financial worry do not of themselves spell peace of mind. And if economies and retrenchment are necessary, let them be taken in good heart. Let one learn courageously to eliminate all but the essential, to remember Thoreau's conviction, that "a man is rich in proportion to the number of things he can afford to leave alone."

It is scientifically, as well as imaginatively, true as the Psalmist said: "The heavens declare the glory of God and the firmament showeth his handiwork." And in the wonder and the majesty of the universe the older person finds relief and comfort and faith. For him, real prayer either frees him from the trouble he fears or else it gives him the strength to meet it when it comes. His religion becomes for him a bulwark, and he finds solace in prayer. Let the oldster echo in his heart the prayer: "Dear God, give us strength to accept with serenity the things that cannot be changed, give us courage to change the things that can and should be changed, and give us wisdom to distinguish the one from the other." The future cannot be bleak and hopeless when he believes. Faith sustains and comforts him.

The wonder and the glory of the world creates an urgency to know, and that urgency—that output of curiosity—is a craving to know. There is in older folk—as in those who are not older—a wide diversity of curiosity both in kind and in vigor.

It would seem that we are in great measure, after all, the architects of our added years. It may, of course, not be in our power to arrange for ourselves good living quarters, a decent living wage; but according to our vision and our health, it is within our power to enrich our later years by maintaining wholesome personal contacts with our fellows and by using our leisure time in some useful activity, no matter how humble, with meaning to ourselves and to others.

There is one thing no retiree can afford to do without— and that is companionship. For that, man has a craving that is never sated. And here, with one's advancing years and loss of friends, and with one's retiring from active work and loss of daily contact with former colleagues, the elderly person is vulnerable. Up to the day of retirement he had enjoyed friendly intercourse with fellow-workers. Now many of these folk whom he still holds dear continue with their absorbing duties. If they come to seek him out, it will be for the reason that the retiree has some powerful attraction—a vital common interest, a merry soul, a congenial master of a mutual hobby, a good host, or a sympathetic friend. If the elderly retiree is not so sought, it behooves him to make himself desirable and interesting to his fellows. Even sheer contentment has the compelling charm of relief. Social concern for the welfare of friends can be a powerful attraction. The oldster must keep alive not only his old friendships, but he must form a circle of new friends with freer hours for inter-course, and consciously he must learn to love and help some younger people so that he can keep in touch with other phases of life's parade than his own. Youth can and should be courted. Youth will, in dividends of grateful affection, pay high for the investment of the oldster's time, interest, and thoughtful attention.

The craving for new experience differs with each indi-vidual. Some persons tragically cease to be curious at twenty; others regrettably at forty; many—and these are the for-tunate ones—never cease to be till death. Yet there are others who cease to look for new experiences. When this happens, senility approaches and the oldster tends to live in his memories, to exalt the past. The doctors call it *misone-ism,* a dislike of and a distaste for something new. This is the cardinal symptom of senility. After it appears and is recognized, it may be already too late to do anything about it. The Chinese proverb tells us, "Learning is like rowing up stream; not to advance is to drop behind."

Dr. Edward L. Bortz, chief of the Medical Services at Lankenau Hospital and past president of the American Medi-cal Association, emphasizes the importance of the aged utilizing the known facts about nutrition, the importance of their avoiding prolonged fatigue, the importance of recrea-tion and sanitation.

Independence—economic and familial—is greatly to be desired, to be planned for, and hopefully to be realized. The man-made tragedy of compulsory retirement has not only deprived many of their work but also of all of its con-comitants—the feeling of contributing to the common weal, the satisfaction that comes of "pulling one's own weight," the comforting conviction that one's work was better done because he did it, the solace of the companionship of fellow-workers—a boon he perhaps never rightfully valued until he lost it—the routine and responsibility of a duty, the pride of family recognition as its financial support, the awareness of social acceptance as a producer, and last, but far from least, the joy that comes of work well done.

Happy is the man or woman who, on growing old, can quickly adjust to necessary changes and find satisfying substitutes; who looks upon retirement from a job, however devoutly served and treasured, as a challenging opportunity for a second career. Happier still will that fortunate person be if this second career expands his circle of friends, raises his sights to service for his fellows, challenges his powers, absorbs his interest, and makes the activities of each day a necessary part of the future he is helping to build for others as well as himself.

Rare indeed is the job that will satisfy all the oldster's needs. Creative activity, however, can supply this sense of achievement. Developing a hobby will challenge one's spare time, conquer (or can happily promote) frustrations, and certainly destroy all sense of loneliness and boredom.

Special centers and Golden Age Clubs can open doors to warm friendships, avenues of reminiscence and pleasurable activities, summer camping, and excursions by bus. Best of all, the public library and the adult school are spurs to action and the building and enjoyment of ever-widening interests. Play, laugh, relax, and enjoy oneself is good medical advice that pays off when followed. We are told that even exercise is not so essential to a happy life as a merry heart, a laugh shared, and "work to do and no work to be done."

In our initial efforts to help retired teachers, we found their financial problem to be the most pressing. It crisscrossed and modified both their attitudes and health. There was a genuine need for adequate income which would eliminate the necessity of their drastically altering their way of life. We believed that the winning of this goal for retired teachers was a realizable one. We also believed that in campaigning for this goal other advantages would accrue to retired teachers: sharing the warmth and fellowship of a worthy crusade, meeting the challenge of faith in one's own endeavors and in the rightness of one's own cause.

Accordingly, in 1947 the National Retired Teachers Association (NRTA) was founded on a shoestring and a prayer. We made no *little* plans, for in little plans lies no magic to stir one's blood. We made big plans. We aimed high in hope and work. We counted upon our people's determination and their missionary spirit. We did not count in vain.

Our little group of retired teachers in California contacted retirees in Connecticut, New York, Ohio, Alabama, Nebraska, and Washington, and together we spearheaded a campaign to attack the inconsistency of two different standards of income taxation—a beneficial one for many employees in private industry and a punitive one for federal employees. The legislative victory of a tax exemption credit of $1200— although not the full goal sought—heightened the tempo of our professional enthusiasm and activity.

Several other challenges of positive service pressed for attention. Housing for the retired was one of these, and 1954 saw the successful opening of Grey Gables, the NRTA residence and headquarters. This we considered an achievement—a retirement residence for the retired, financed and administered without subsidy by the retired. Grey Gables is a charming country-club type of residence, in a small urban location, a town proud of its cultural offerings and appreciative of both Grey Gables and its membership. Here 82 men and women have built a tradition of gracious living. By life-lease payments they provide themselves with a place for pleasant and friendly associations and activities, and they have endowed it with a priceless ingredient—a cheerful attitude of mutual regard and living.

In 1955 NRTA successfully ended its five-year campaign for hospital-surgical insurance protection. This protection, now available to all members, is without medical examination or age limitations and covers pre-existing ailments. For the 65'ers this victory constituted a break-through of the insurance barrier. Since the inception of this plan other insurance plans for 65'ers have been offered, but the NRTA offering, increasing each year in benefits without increase of premium, is still the most liberal in the field. Currently, added provisions are being made, including post-operative care in licensed nursing homes, payment for prescribed drugs, and increased payments over extended time for hospital room and board.

With the successful termination of many state-wide campaigns for retirement benefits, some of our membership asked us to help them secure at budget-prices European travel opportunities. Travel Service, Incorporated, a non-profit organization, answered this need. In the summer of 1958 NRTA sent on a leisurely, professionally conducted tour over 300 members. In the summer of 1959, 500 men and women were visiting the Mediterranean, Scandinavia, or taking the "Grand Circle Tour." In 1960 the Orient beckons.

Each year has seen our organization achieve one or more goals; yet there are other goals requiring long-term effort. Among these are:

Legislation further improving retirement provisions and removing retirement inequities.

The wider adoption of permission for substitute teaching without jeopardy to retirement benefits.

The need on the part of state legislatures to keep retirement benefits paralleling the spiraling costs of living.

Death benefits to cover funeral costs—a benefit already guaranteed in some states.

Associational cooperation, on all levels, with organizations having similar goals.

The expansion of our housing program.

The expansion of counseling service.

The improvement of our publication, the *NRTA Journal,* which has won the proud distinction of selling its jokes to *Coronet!*

The enthusiasm of our membership—grown to nearly 100,000 persons—was so great, particularly for the benefits of its insurance protection, that we were urged in 1958 to aid those retirees not eligible for NRTA membership. We met this demand by founding an affiliated non-profit organization, open to all older persons, and offering its members benefits similar to those offered by the older NRTA organization. Announcement of the founding of this organization was made in the bi-monthly publication *Modern Maturity,* and the new group was named The American Association of Retired Persons.

The need for such a unifying association is proved by its growth, in only nine months, to 50,000 strong. Gracious recognition has come to it from official sources, such as HEW, the Veterans' Administration, and the Congressional Committees interested in problems of the aged and aging. Enthusiastic members send word as to its success in bringing to them a feeling of cheer and companionship, and of faith in the future. Here is a note I recently received:

Modern Maturity just received. Wonderfully informative, inspirational, helpful, and beautiful—a work of art. You and your staff are to be congratulated . . . an excellent publication for those who, in their declining years, are still no less desirous of a place in the sun. . . . This tribute is from one who practically wasted two precious years, bemoaning the seeming fact that life *ends* at eighty.

In September 1959, there opened for the members of NRTA and AARP our first nursing home, The Acacias, which was modeled architecturally upon nearby Grey Gables. It is dedicated to the service and welfare of our members who need the professional care, comfort, and attention of a health center.

Important as was the opening of this first health center, we feel that a plan to meet the needs of the other thousands of ailing oldsters by a substantial reduction in the cost of medicines is of no less importance. At the present moment the NRTA and AARP are cooperating in a plan whereby nationally known medicines or prescriptions by licensed physicians filled by licensed pharmacists are to be sold to the aged through regional offices. Once again our two organizations are demonstrating their unceasing effort to improve life for all the nation's people over 65.

Mens sana in corpore sano. This is our answer to those of our thoughtful members who remind us "of the extraordinary power for good which is inherent in the retired group," and that our program is "wonderfully conceived to carry out the ideals and functions of maturity of thought, maturity of experience, and maturity of judgment." We feel humble before the spiritual reserves within the retired group which make for a deep yearning for a betterment in government and world understanding. To release this expression is one of the objectives of *Modern Maturity*.

We all know that we shall grow old, yet we do not plan for the meaningful continuation of the interests essential to our happiness; we vaguely imagine retirement will offer opportunities for catching up with the unrealized dreams of yesteryear, yet we are likely to fear and postpone building the foundations for their positive realizations.

Surely, in spite of all other conditions and factors, success in retirement is largely what the individual makes it. Negative feelings can be converted into positive experiences for graceful aging, but it largely depends upon how well the oldster can adjust to change and philosophically accept his waning powers. How he will do this depends in turn upon his capacity to see humor and express it, to enjoy a chuckle at his own follies and forgive his own shortcomings and those of his intimates and, very importantly, to have the conviction that he is called upon to render service.

Dr. Paul D. Moody is quoted as saying, "The measure of a man is not in the number of his servants but in the number of people he serves." The oldster who loves his family, who shares, with his neighbor, of his time and of himself, who helps his community become a happier, healthier place because he is in it, is truly successful. For him, aging ceases to be a problem—he has become the answer to it.

THE REFUGEE

By ALIDA DE JAGER

The homeless, jobless, citizenless, driven from their native lands by authoritarian tyranny—the refugees and escapees—are "neighbors" to Alida de Jager.

ALIDA DE JAGER has literally lived and breathed refugee assistance for almost fifteen years. Daughter of a prominent Dutch Socialist, her schooling near Paris was interrupted by the war in 1940 when she escaped with her family first to England and then to Mexico. After the war she returned to England and started work in the refugee field. Moving to Geneva in 1946, she became, first a welfare counselor, and later a director, for the International Rescue Committee, an American voluntary agency.

For twelve years Miss de Jager participated both in the theoretical work of various Geneva conferences and in practical refugee work throughout Europe. IRC Geneva, under her direction, brought to Switzerland hundreds of former concentration camp inmates from Germany, Austria, and France for more or less prolonged hospitalization, sent thousands of food parcels to the war-stricken countries, arranged for the emigration to the United States of many refugees without hope of resettlement in Europe. It administered Reparation Fund moneys for assistance and resettlement of Nazi-victims and drafted many refugee projects.

Miss de Jager was instrumental in creating a home for pre-tubercular children in Switzerland, took part in organizing emergency relief for Hungarian refugees in Austria, helped arrange scholarship grants to refugee students, and succeeded in placing permanently in Western countries young unaccompanied Hungarians who presented a special problem after the revolution in 1958. She served as European representative of the Zellerbach Commission study on the European refugee situation. No friend of almsgiving and long worried lest the plight of the individual refugee be lost sight of, she has aimed constantly at finding practical, constructive solutions to encourage and enable refugees to become self-supporting and independent.

The Refugee

*F*OURTEEN years after the end of World War II, while the Western world has virtually recovered economically, there are still some 130,000 unsettled refugees from totalitarian countries in Western Europe. Some 30,000 are living in camps* and the rest, little or no better off, in slums and dismal hovels.

[In addition to these European refugees, there are approximately a million Arab refugees in the Middle East receiving minimum assistance from the United Nations Relief and Works Agency; another million from the Chinese mainland living in poverty in Hong Kong with almost 10,000 European refugees still on the mainland; over 150,000 Algerian refugees in North Africa; plus Tibetan refugees in India and Nepal, Chinese refugees in Southeast Asia, refugees from

* A report in November 1959, by the UN High Commissioner for Refugees indicated that this figure was down to 22,000 and that the impact of World Refugee Year (July 1, 1959-June 30, 1960) had awakened new hopes among the refugees.—Ed.

Egypt—all adding up to more than two million displaced homeless persons.—Ed.]

Looking back upon many years of work among the refugees in Europe, our forgotten neighbors, memories surge up.

It is raining. An icy wind is blowing on the Austro-Hungarian frontier. The night is very dark. Somewhere in the distance shots are heard. But the Hungarian frontier guards are not shooting at their escaping brothers, they are emptying their rifles into the air in order to demonstrate their vigilance to the Russian soldiers further back.

Sometimes in groups, sometimes one by one, men, women, and children are coming across the bare fields—exhausted and frozen. Only a few carry bags; most of them took nothing on their flight. They left all their belongings behind: their homes, their country, their family, their friends. But their faces are shining. They embrace the Austrians waiting for them. Some kneel down and kiss the soil. They have escaped. They are free. And freedom is more precious to them than all they left behind.

Two hundred thousand escaped to Austria and Yugo-slavia. The Hungarian Exodus . . . For once the world is shaken. People are roused from their inertia. Help is forthcoming immediately. Red tape is abolished. Overseas and European countries open wide their doors. Within ten months 170,000 Hungarian refugees are received by the free world. And not only received, they are accepted as equals, given a home and the right to work.

But even this great and generous impetus ebbs after some time. A small backlog is left over. Today, more than two years after the Hungarian revolution, 5,700 are still in Austrian camps, among them some 600 handicapped and some 200 children and youth under 17 years of age who escaped

without their parents. Will theirs be the same fate as that of
the "old refugees" stagnating in camps ever since the war?

How much bitterness did these "old refugees" feel, when
they witnessed the Hungarian newcomers receiving all they
had waited for in vain year after year? What could I say to
the Hungarian refugee in Camp Landshut, Bavaria, who
escaped from his country in 1949 under infinitely more difficult conditions than the post-revolt Hungarians? He was one
of the few who succeeded in crossing alive the mined
frontier fields. He had been an active anti-Communist and
had risked his life to reach the free world. The free world?
Ten years in a stone cell, worse than prison, because in
prison you atone for a crime and you can look forward to
release, while he and his companions are punished for having believed in Western ideals and by now have lost all hope
in a different life. They were left behind in camp because
immigration authorities took exception to a long-healed scar
on the lung, or because their professional skill was not in
demand, or because one had once been a member of the
Communist Party, a taint which neither subsequent resistance nor flight can erase.

The children of these refugees have been born here and
know nothing but camp existence. Theirs is misery and utter
despair. They have ceased to be human beings. They are
living dead, vegetating from day to day.

Visiting commissions, officials, social workers say: "They
are drunkards, you cannot help them any more. Whatever
you do for them is wasted." They are "irrecuperables."
According to statistics 40 per cent of them can no longer be
integrated into normal life. But these statistics err. They take
no account of the invincible vitality of man. I dare contend
that many, very many of these men and women, condemned

by our indifference, could become useful and self-supporting citizens again, if we accepted them as our neighbors, if we gave them back their human dignity, not necessarily by costly and elaborate projects, but by giving them a home, the possibility to work, and a friend to lean on.

Ventures like Galvania in Austria and Beckhof in Germany, among others, go far to prove this.

The Galvania project near Salzburg was started by two Latvian refugees, Messrs. Razinski and Knuski, who had been rejected for emigration, one because his wife was an invalid, the other because he had once suffered from tuberculosis. Mr. Knuski is an engineer specializing in cold galvanization of metals, a process little known in Austria. Their project was sponsored by the World Council of Churches, the UN High Commissioner for Refugees, and the U.S. Escapee Program. They succeeded in setting up a factory, employing other refugees who on account of physical handicaps had been refused their emigration visa. Thanks to this project 30 so-called "hard-core" refugees have become self-supporting again.

The Beckhof settlement near Bielefeld is mainly the achievement of two men, a clergyman, the Rev. Mr. Abakuks, in whose mind the idea was born, and Mr. W. Gebauer, who with untiring energy, devotion, and competence carried it out and created this model community where 220 refugees, everyone of them given up as hopeless—maimed, paralytics, mentally disturbed, nearly blind—are today earning their livelihood. Local firms also became interested in training handicapped refugees to produce items that required little experience or expenditure of physical energy such as gluing suitcases, assembling washing machine pumps and vacuum cleaners, etc.

Mr. Gebauer says:

Our work with these people was preceded by months of psychological attention. We visited the foreign refugees in their camp surroundings. Close personal contacts were established. They told us about the things they had lived through, their needs and worries. We went on excursions together and arranged social events in camp; we invited German groups, women's clubs, and newspaper men to join us with the twofold purpose of overcoming psychological resistance and of dispelling mutual distrust and prejudices.

If I were to tell you the history of our institution over the last four years, much of it would sound like a work of fiction. Often we were close to breaking down because the refugees had relapsed into their earlier failings, the worst of which were alcoholism and total listlessness. Nevertheless we persevered. Again and again we had to persuade them to go back to work, until something in them gradually changed. Somehow, the will to live was reborn in them and they came to desire work because they realized its manifold benefits.

We consulted not only the medical specialists and the psychologists, but also the clergymen, the work supervisors and colleagues of the patient. Each case had to be individually handled.

For those physically unable to do any other work, a "philatelic department" was set up at Beckhof, receiving from all over the world envelopes from which refugees wash off the stamps and classify them for sale. The director of this department, himself a refugee, writes:

Here people from seven different nations come together, emerging from neglect and despair, to show the world that they can still do useful work, in spite of their illness. The stamp department started with five people and five kilograms of unwashed stamps. Five people—five different nations. One might think a new Babel. But the contrary happened: the workshop has become a little UN. Here there are no more frontiers or hostile nationalism—only human beings. Here they sit together, in friendship and peace, at tables burdened with stamps—a Latvian officer with a Rumanian peasant from the Bukovina, a Russian secondary school teacher with a Yugoslav forest guard.

No case is hopeless, unless we give up.

Athens, cradle of our civilization—luminous abode of the gods. The sun is sparkling on white marble columns, symbols of the serene beauty of classic art. Thousands of visitors are breathlessly taking in the unequalled beauty of the ancient sites. But no sun penetrates the former tobacco factory of Kolokinthou on the outskirts of Athens. Nowhere in Europe do people live under such dismal conditions as here and in the other refugee camps in Greece. Their inmates are mostly Greek nationals who lived all their lives in countries now under totalitarian rule, such as Rumania, Bulgaria, Russia, China, and so on. They escaped and returned to their homeland which was itself too poor to offer them a new existence.

The big halls of the former factory have been separated into "boxes" with old carpets or curtains made from rags. There is no ventilation or heating. Bad odors and noise are all-pervading. The old and the sick, sufferers from TB, paralysis, hysteria, and other illnesses, mingle with children and babies. Families of four to seven, including parents, children, and grandparents, have from ten to fifteen square meters at their disposal. Here they live, love, sleep, cook, and dry their laundry. Food is insufficient. The children are undernourished. Eighty per cent are pretubercular.

A boy, following us as we leave, shouts: "Look at us! We are no longer human beings! Why do you keep us here?"

Jesus said, "Let the children come to me for of such is the kingdom of God." But our democratic, Christian world ignores their plight. If we lived up to the truth, we would have to do something or to avow that our attitude is: "Let these children live in hell and die, for we do not care."

Years and years ago, but now long forgotten, there was another exodus strangely similar to the Hungarian one.

450,000 Spanish refugees crossed the Pyrenees to France, leaving their country after a hopeless fight against a dictator supported with arms and men by the German and Italian totalitarian regimes of that time. Crowded by the tens of thousands in enormous camps in Southern France, many of them took up arms again to fight for France when the Second World War broke out. Those who were captured by the Germans were considered not as prisoners of war but interned in concentration camps.

Antonio, one of them, brought in a hopeless condition to a Swiss sanatorium by the Red Cross at the end of the war, rediscovered with childlike amazement the life and traffic in the streets of a small Swiss town. He had not seen anything like this since his childhood in Spain. From 1937 to 1939 he had been interned in the camp at Argeles in Southern France. Then, he had enrolled in the French Army and had been captured by the Germans and jailed in Dachau concentration camp. Liberated by the allies, he was in a sanatorium for three years more. Hopelessly ill with TB and diabetes, the voluntary agency caring for him published his picture in a publicity pamphlet under the heading, "He must die." But Antonio did not die. He married and is working in a factory. True, every year or two he has a relapse of his old illness and has to go to a sanatorium again. But even so he is among the lucky ones. He is not one of the 25,000 who died for France in the war or of the 5,000 who came back permanently maimed, nor one of those who in despair left the French camps in 1938 to go to Russia and are today in Siberian camps, all efforts to get in touch with them or get them out having failed, nor one of the thousands still living at present in utter destitution in France.

Another refugee among the very privileged was Ferdinand Hardekopf. A well-known German writer and poet, he es-

caped from Hitler-Germany to France. During the German
occupation he and his wife went into hiding. After the war
they managed to reach that island of peace and well-being,
Switzerland. In 1947, as today, refugees in German and
Austrian camps, would have considered it a great bliss to
live freely, within their own four walls in that dream country, be it even in a garret, receiving from the Swiss government and voluntary agencies a monthly allowance preclud-
ing actual hunger, although nothing remained for the
amenities of life.

But the Hardekopfs were not accepted as neighbors. Had
they been given the right and the possibility to work instead
of having to ask for alms, they would have managed to carry
on. Yet they put up a brave fight. She was ill and needed
special care which could not be provided from their meager
allowance. Nobody cared.

"My wife is very ill. We two helpless ones are forsaken.
My loneliness is not bearable any more," Hardekopf wrote
me in December 1953. Four weeks later he tried to commit
suicide. According to Swiss law, would-be-suicides are committed to mental institutions. Here Hardekopf contracted
pneumonia. A few weeks later he died in the general ward,
surrounded by lunatics. His wife, left alone, carried on for
a few months. Then she jumped from a window. More
successful than her husband, she died instantly.

A kaleidoscope. A few episodes out of thousands. All those
perished and yet could have lived if we had accepted them
as neighbors. And all those who still can be saved, if we do
not consider them as embarrassing undesirables, but as our
brothers, who, without their guilt, by circumstances beyond
their control, or by active defense of our ideals of freedom,
came into their present plight. They preferred uncertainty
and want to a normal life under totalitarian rule in their

own country. They were willing to give up everything for freedom and they found barbed wires.

Much is being done by governmental, intergovernmental, and private agencies, but much more is needed to solve the problem. No new organizations, administrations, speeches, and promises, but the preparedness of a few countries to receive their share of the remaining refugees in Europe and the willingness of the people of these countries to accept the refugees as neighbors.

THE

SEGREGATED

By RICHARD AMBROSE REEVES

Those discriminated against because of color, and denied freedom and education by the apartheid policies in South Africa, are "neighbors" to Ambrose Reeves.

THE RT. REV. RICHARD AMBROSE REEVES, Bishop of Johannesburg, is chief pastor of one of the most complex and turbulent dioceses of the Anglican Communion. As a Lancashire parish priest and later as a canon of Liverpool Cathedral, he spent much time among the Liverpool dockers and helped to mediate the 1945 dock strike. Believing that the Christian life should embrace all spheres of social activity, today he is a leader of a Church facing persecution for its staunch opposition to the racial segregation policies of the South African Government.

Since his consecration as Bishop of Johannesburg in 1949, he has championed the cause of the underprivileged and dispossessed, taking a leading part in the demand for better housing for African workers in Johannesburg and strongly opposing the Government's cancellation of African freehold rights in Sophiatown and the compulsory removal of Africans elsewhere. When the Bantu Education Act passed in 1956, Bishop Reeves closed the mission schools in his diocese rather than hand them over to the Government; when the Government arrested 161 citizens of all races, political beliefs, and religious affiliations on a charge of high treason, Bishop Reeves organized a Treason Trial Defense Fund to insure adequate legal representation for those arrested and care for their families; when, in January, 1957, over 60,000 Africans went on strike against the increase in Johannesburg bus fares, he mediated discussions between the strikers and bus lines, successfully negotiating a settlement whereby Johannesburg employers paid the difference of the increased fare; when, in April, 1957, the Assembly passed the Native Laws Amendment Bill forbidding Africans to worship in churches in areas set aside for white people, he and the other bishops of the Anglican Church of South Africa stated that they would be unable to obey this law or advise their people to do the same.

More recently, the Bishop has been greatly concerned with the appalling conditions of labor on some of the farms in the Transvaal, and early in 1959 he became chairman of a committee of fourteen organizations which meets regularly for consultation and joint action on limited civic and social objectives.

The Segregated

FEW WORDS in the English language are responsible for more violent emotional reactions than the word "race." It arouses people's prejudices, loyalties, animosities, and fears, particularly in those countries in the world in which a dominant white group lives in close proximity to other ethnic groups. Among such areas is South Africa, which, while it has no monopoly of racial tension in the modern world, is confronted by this great unsolved problem of color in a form which is probably more acute than that experienced in any other country. Not that this problem has been created by the present South African Government. It has been the most pressing problem for the members of every racial group in South Africa ever since the arrival of the white man; in the very early days the white man struggled for survival, later he struggled for the possession of the land, and when he had secured control of the country, he devised ways and means to ensure that the vast black population should be kept in a position of subservience. So, historically, there has been a long succession of laws which prevented the African from obtaining the franchise and from owning land except in the reserves. In industry and commerce, legislation has enforced a rigid color-bar which has made it extremely difficult for the African to develop his skills. And in order to make certain that he remained subservient to the white man he has been subjected to the pass system and service contracts.

All this was an integral part of the social structure of South Africa long years before the National Party came into power. Truly it was claimed that this was a policy of trustee-ship, but the trouble was that those in successive govern-ments neither devoted much time nor money to the millions of people whom they regarded as their wards, nor did they seem to consider that such trusteeship at best could only be transitory, for wards are bound to become adults. It is small wonder that such a policy brought disillusionment and frus-tration to growing numbers of Africans.

The situation was already far from satisfactory when the present Government came into power some ten years ago. Immediately they began to put their racial theory of seg-regation into practice, and it is the effect of what has been happening in these last years which has lessons that ought to be learned by those in every land who are faced by this same issue.

In these last ten years there has been a spate of legislation designed to give effect to this dogma of differential develop-ment; laws which have been concerned with tightening the Pass Laws, giving the government greater powers against African leaders, taking away what little freehold title Afri-cans previously had in urban areas, and controlling the African population in rural and urban areas outside the reserves. In addition, we have had such laws as the Bantu Education Act, the Universities and Nursing Acts, as well as the Industrial Conciliation Act and the Native Laws Amendment Act. All this has been carried through in obedience to the policy of apartheid.

The meaning of this word "apartheid" is clear for it means "apartness" or "segregation." The difficulty arises when anyone seeks to give this word content, because it can imply such very different things to different people, as can be seen from the statement issued by the Afrikaans intellectuals in the South African Bureau of Racial Affairs, the report of the Socio-Economic Commission, the legislation enacted by the present South African Government, and the opinions of the average South African on this issue. Yet however varied may be the definition that is given to "apartheid" by different groups and individuals, all such definitions rest upon the assumption that the white and non-white groups are racially and culturally incompatible and for this reason must be kept apart at all cost, even though the cost is so great that no society can afford indefinitely to meet it unless it is willing to face financial bankruptcy and moral collapse.

As Prof. C. W. de Kiewiet says in his book, *The Anatomy of South African Misery:*

In its various forms apartheid is a transfer of the responsibilities of the living world to a dream world of solved problems. It is the substitution of a wishful simplicity for a real complexity. The basic premise of apartheid is that the natives can seek no remedies and gain no citizenship within white society, but only within their own segregated society. It is at this critical point that the remarkably well-written documents issued by S.A.B.R.A. step from fact into make-believe, using a dextrous logic to brush aside history and economics . . . They do indeed invoke economic and political principles, but they are the principles of a non-existent world, so that their scholarship becomes spurious and their logic a delusion . . . Under the guise of hope and deliverance the formula of apartheid is a creed of despair and a flight from the fearfulness of the real problem . . . It is a vision of a false and unattainable utopia imposed upon a native population that does not aspire to it.

I have quoted somewhat extensively from de Kiewiet's words, because if they are true of the intellectual, high-minded, and sincere apostles of complete apartheid, how completely do they expose the hypocrisy of a government that in fact is only concerned with preserving white domination. And if they are true, as I am convinced they are, how shoddy and disreputable do they make the attitude to this matter of so many white South Africans. Truly the history of South Africa during the last three centuries provides an abundant explanation of why so many people champion the racial ideology of apartheid, and why many more cling to it desperately. The social, economic, and political distinctions in South Africa are the logical results of the relationship established by those white men who came to the country in the heyday of colonial expansion. But the snare and delusion from which their successors have suffered is a belief that a social order can be preserved which their own economic activities are destroying. The black man is learning the ways of commerce and industry with which he is confronted by the white man. In consequence, he is struggling to rise above the old tribal ways so that he may take his place as a member of a civilized community. How rapidly this is taking place can be seen from the fact that in the last thirty-five years the number of Africans in urban areas has quadrupled. Further, in spite of all the legislation to halt and reverse this process the numbers are steadily rising. If this does not succeed in persuading anyone of the stupidity of such a policy, he has only to recall that the authors of the Tomlinson Report, issued by the commission set up to deal with this very problem, estimate that even if their recommendations were to be implemented immediately, there would be three times as many Africans in the urban areas by the end of this century as there are at the present moment. No wonder that in spite of a flood of legislation aimed at maintaining the status quo, white people in South Africa feel insecure and are afraid. The tragedy is that they still pin their faith on segregation in one form or another, blissfully ignorant that it can only work outside history and economics, for it has no relevance to the contemporary world.

As will be expected, such a policy is having serious moral consequences. To estimate the moral effects of segregation certain moral standards must be established against which such consequences are to be measured. For myself, the only standard by which an attempt can be made to evaluate this is the Christian ethic as that ethic is set forth in the New Testament. There it is clear beyond all argument that the God of the Christians is the God of the whole world; that the Good News of the love of God is for all peoples; that once an individual is incorporated into the Body of Christ in Holy Baptism he finds himself in a brotherhood in which all differences of race, color, and class are transcended. In short, the emphasis is laid both upon the value of the individual and upon his capacity to live in Christ in charity with others in such a way that a unity is created which is entirely other than that collectivism which is so fashionable in an age in which totalitarian claims are being made by the state. In the Christian community individuals retain their individual differences, their specialized gifts, and their particular capacities, but they use them all as expression of their corporate life.

It is for this reason that Christians are compelled to declare that whatever form apartheid may take, it is completely opposed to the spirit of Christianity. It doesn't matter whether it is sincerely intended to separate the people into exclusively black or white areas, or is pursued as the only way of preserving white domination, it is contrary to the teaching of the New Testament. To say this is not for one moment to ignore the dangers that beset white South Africans, especially in the present situation in South Africa. Still less ought it to be suggested that such a policy of segregation is so utterly immoral that it can be written off as a complete loss. To do that would be completely irresponsible, for the consequences of human actions are rarely completely evil, just as they are never completely good, however high a person's intentions may be. At the same time the moral cost upon both Africans and Europeans is tremendous. Anyone who is continually in intimate contact with Africans cannot fail to realize how serious is the moral cost to the Africans in so many ways, for neither have they been consulted about the steps taken to implement this policy nor have they any desire to live in a watertight compartment cut off from western civilization. There is the mounting hatred that increasing numbers of Africans have for the police. It is true that this may be misplaced because the police force is under orders. Nevertheless it is a fact, and it may have the gravest consequences for the whole community when, as in South Africa at the present time, a large section of the population come to regard the guardians of the law and order as their enemies. Then there is the resentment of numbers of parents who are compelled against their will either to accept Bantu Education or who cannot get any education at all for their children. Then there is the frustration of masses of workers who move beween mean homes and work which offers no prospect of improving their position, and the dangerous anger of African leaders who have no means of political expression. Hatred, resentment, frustration, and anger are all qualities of the human mind and heart, the very things with which morality has to deal and which morals exist to combat. Added to all this are the constant and alarming crimes against life and property committed by Africans, which are a constant anxiety in the towns and cities of South Africa. There is little hope that such a sorry state of affairs will be remedied while Africans find themselves constantly arrested for the most trivial offenses. As many as 600,000 Africans are imprisoned each year, of which more than half are for offenses against the Pass Laws and the Liquor Laws. Today in South Africa apartheid is breeding these evil things on a grand scale in the minds and hearts of countless thousands of Africans. Certainly the moral effects of this great experiment in segregation are such that a great moral debit balance is being rapidly built up in the African people.

But grievous as have been the moral results of the policies of the last few years upon the non-Europeans, the moral effects that such policies are having upon many white people in South Africa are even more disturbing. There has, I believe, been a noticeable loss in integrity among Europeans in recent times. This shows itself in a great variety of ways: in the alarming rise in prison statistics; in the prevalence of juvenile delinquency; in the growth in drunkenness and loose living; in the increasing breakdown in family life; in a general deterioration in the standards of conduct, courtesy, and good manners which are so noticeable. It would be an exaggeration to link all this too closely with the policy of compulsory segregation, but there is a closer connection between public policies and personal behavior than is sometimes suspected. More than that, the student of history knows that the past provides many examples of the evil effects upon a ruling class which has determined at all costs to retain all the power in its own hands. Perhaps it will only be when it is too late to affect the situation that the Europeans in South Africa will realize that the moral cost of these last years has been so tremendous that they have become seriously morally impoverished as a result.

Still, to speak so of the moral consequences of apartheid

unfortunately does not exhaust the full account of its effects. Perhaps the historians of the future will conclude that the greatest moral failure of the moment has been that the great majority of those who have the political power to influence the course of events have used all their strength to maintain a rigid political and social structure in a rapidly changing society. That would not be a very grave indictment if there was any chance of it being successful. But the long story of mankind suggests that if it did succeed it would be a unique instance of a small ruling minority imposing its will indefinitely on a hostile majority. The serious thing from the moral point of view is that such action must inevitably lead to the destruction of many valuable social institutions which have been built up so laboriously through the years, whereas this time could have been so usefully employed in transforming them in such a fashion that they would have continued to serve the needs of this rapidly changing multiracial society.

Yet it is not only the moral consequences of compulsory segregation which have to be taken into account, for when the financial aspect of apartheid is examined, the position is found to be just as disturbing. If the changeover from an agrarian to an industrial economy is to proceed satisfactorily, there must be a steady increase in the number of skilled technicians who are available for industry and commerce and a trained labor force that is able to exploit to the full the tremendous possibilities of development that result from scientific research and mechanical inventions. The former calls for an attractive immigration policy that will ensure that South Africa receives its fair share of skilled personnel. This is the very reverse of what is happening in spite of the high salaries offered and the many undoubted advantages of climate and living standards that obtain in the Union. For example, the number of South Africans emigrating to

Canada has trebled in the last few years. The probability is that the number is small, but it is an indication of what is taking place. Indeed there is small doubt that if the present situation continues, the time will come when we shall find that the number of white people leaving the country will exceed the number coming to settle. Even now the shortage of highly skilled manpower is a more serious matter than the shortage of capital, grave as that undoubtedly is. But even more serious is the fact that four-fifths of our population is inefficient, unskilled, and uneducated. The newcomer to South Africa is impressed by the fact that the Union has so much and such cheap labor at the disposal of industry and commerce. But he will not be in the country very long before he comes to the conclusion that far from it being cheap, it is the most expensive labor in any industrialized community in the modern world just because it is so ignorant and untrained. Further, the fact that urban Africans have no real stake at all in the urban community means that there is a continual turnover in the labor forces of most establishments which is extremely costly, to say nothing of the malnutrition from which many workers suffer and the growing spirit of resentment among African urban workers which still further impairs their efficiency. It is sometimes maintained that the lot of the African in South Africa is so much better than it is in so many other African territories. But true as this may be in terms of money, it takes no account of the fact that unlike so many of these other territories we are rapidly becoming a great industrial community. It might be more profitable, for example, to compare South Africa with a rapidly developing country such as Canada, for if that were done, we should discover that while the Union has four-fifths of Canada's population it has only one-fifth of its national income. The plain fact is that South Africa cannot continue to afford the luxury of compulsory segregation unless it is prepared to face the possibility of economic disaster.

From intimate and continual contact with the African leadership during the bus boycott of 1957, it seems to me that whatever laws may be passed to preserve the status quo in South Africa, nothing will be able to prevent the recurrence of acts of resistance and protest such as were seen during that struggle. The danger is that the very laws which are intended to secure segregation will only succeed in ensuring that the leadership of the African people passes into more extreme and irresponsible hands as increasing numbers of responsible and moderate leaders are arrested or banned from taking any part in African political life. Already there are signs that antagonism to the authorities is passing over into antagonism to all white people. What the outcome will be is difficult to discern, for it is almost impossible to predict what may happen. Without attempting to predict the course of future events in such a confused and complex situation, the events of these last years have demonstrated all too plainly that the present policy of establishing separate racial communities in South Africa is fraught with tremendous danger, if not disaster, for all who live in that land. Somehow, the peoples in South Africa have to reestablish confidence in race relationships, and take the road of co-operation, instead of segregation, before it is too late. It is only as white, black, and Coloured recognize that they have been set in one country to learn to live together as neighbors in a multi-racial society that they have any future. The road of neighborliness is a much harder road to travel than that which is at present being followed, but there is no other way in which confidence can be re-established both between the various ethnic groups within South Africa and also between South Africa and the other peoples in the Western world.

THE
MEDICALLY
UNDER-
PRIVILEGED

By GORDON S. SEAGRAVE

Those living in the rugged hills of
Burma with no knowledge of modern
medical care, suspicious of doctors
and surgery and medicines, are
"neighbors" to Gordon Seagrave.

GORDON S. SEAGRAVE, the famous Burma surgeon, has spent 37 years bringing modern medical treatment to North Burma and neighboring China. Born in Burma of American missionary parents, he has devoted his life to that country. After graduating from Denison University, he completed his medical training at Johns Hopkins University in 1920.

Until World War II Dr. Seagrave worked in the Northern Shan States only a few miles from the China border and founded the Namkham Hospital, long the center of his work in fighting against malaria, tuberculosis, dysentery, plague, rickets, and a score of other diseases.

During the war years when Japanese invaders broke into Burma, Dr. Seagrave served in the Medical Corps under General Stilwell, caring for American and Chinese sick and wounded with his devoted Burmese nurses.

In 1950, with Communist China threatening the Burmese border and the Karen tribesmen in open rebellion, Dr. Seagrave was charged with treason to the Burmese Republic for being over-friendly with the Karens. After a year of litigation and detention in a Rangoon jail for many months, he obtained complete vindication from the Supreme Court of Burma. Despite the hardships and illness of two years' imprisonment, Dr. Seagrave went back immediately to the rugged Shan hills and restored his nurses training school. Today thousands of patients from all parts of the country seek him out at Namkham Hospital.

Dr. Seagrave is the author of many articles and books, including *Waste-Basket Surgeon, Burma Surgeon,* and *Burma Surgeon Returns.*

The Medically Underprivileged

I WAS born among the medically underprivileged of Burma and have spent most of my life here. In fact, it was to serve these people that I studied medicine. My mother had almost finished her studies in the Woman's Medical School in Philadelphia when she was struck down by typhoid and my father made her quit. But in Rangoon she set up a little dispensary and did what she could for the local inhabitants who could not get attention at the Rangoon General Hospital. Many patients came to her from the jungles of the Irrawaddy Delta and, as I hung on to her apron strings—I was the youngest in the fourth generation of the family to work for Burma—I learned so much about human physical misery that I never changed for one instant my decision to become a doctor and do something about it. While I was a college student in Ohio, the example of Zwemer in Arabia and of Cort in Thailand kept my zeal white hot. At Johns Hopkins Grenfell, and his work for the people of Labrador, inspired me so much that I was almost

163

tempted to go to Labrador instead of returning to my first and last love, Burma. For the last twenty years Schweitzer of Africa has been my inspiration—and has continually made me ashamed of my moments of weakness. The world owes a great deal to these great men.

When I came back to Burma as a doctor, medical work for the Burmese was done only by the Government and the missions. The Government, as governments always must, began its work in the cities and then spread out slowly towards the villages. Its work never reached out into the wilder jungles. The mission hospitals were also in the cities. In outlying areas the missions had only dispensaries under qualified medical men. The idea was to use medicine to obtain converts for the churches. The result was a failure—not many conversions nor many cures were obtained; certainly not cures of really serious illness. These dispensaries have now been abandoned.

Even so, the missions were about fifty years ahead of their times. They were private institutions working for the people with private funds voluntarily contributed by individuals, either from abroad or from within the country itself, often by people who could hardly afford to spare any money at all.

It was World War II and the misery which followed that first initiated direct government assistance for the sick, and the international programs of WHO and UNICEF. This foreign aid was used to wipe out the mass scourges of malaria, leprosy, venereal disease, and malnutrition; but most people were still without help when it came to the illnesses that affected their day-to-day living: broken bones, eye diseases, acute and chronic surgical conditions, and even childbirth. In instances such as these they had to depend upon government hospitals or upon institutions supported by person-to-person gifts. It is through these private institutions that Americans—who not so long ago were themselves medically underprivileged—can best assist in abolishing the physical misery in which millions live.

When the Namkham Hospital began, it was a mission institution receiving a token grant-in-aid from the government. The hospital grew to be an institution of a hundred beds in two stone buildings and supported with funds secured from abroad as well as from the people of Burma. It was when the Government saw that this work was successful that grants-in-aid were given toward the cost of further expansion. Some of these grants were made before the war, but most were contributed during the first post-war years. Nowadays the Government, concerned with developing its own institutions, can spare little to help other deserving hospitals. What it can spare is given to improve the quality of treatment rather than to help in further expansion, no matter how essential that expansion may be. Since the demand for medical care has tripled during the last five years, Namkham will have to depend on person-to-person assistance for a long time to come.

Under British rule, Burma had, before World War II, developed a fairly large number of hospitals, some of which were well-staffed. Certainly Burma was better off than Laos where, I am told, there is only one fully qualified native doctor for a population of two million people. That could be a world's record. Yet, in 1948, when Prime Minister U Nu told me that Burma had the highest infant mortality of any country in the world, I was shocked. Why I was shocked, I don't know, for at Namkham we always asked every woman how many children she had had and how many had lived, and these case histories invariably showed that many had had from six to fifteen children of whom none, or just one or two, had lived.

Infant mortality has appalled me ever since I started my

work here in Burma thirty-seven years ago. To meet the problem, I had, from the beginning, urged every pregnant woman who came to us for any reason to have her baby in the hospital and to come to us early so that we could give her proper prenatal care. The first woman who came, however—she had already been in labor seven days and the baby dead for the last three days—was promptly divorced by her husband for having come. The situation became easier after I graduated my first group of nurse-midwives and let it be known that I would take the nurse-midwife to a patient's home, remain outside, and not interfere unless the case proved to be an abnormal one which the nurse could not handle. We refused to take money from any maternity case—thereby insulting quite a few who felt shamed if we did not accept a donation.

Perhaps it was a good thing when I was sent to jail on suspicion in 1950. My jail term put Namkham on the map, and during the past seven years not only have abnormal obstetric cases come to us from very long distances—sometimes three- or four-days journey—but also a great many women have come equal distances to have their first baby born here and their others as well.

I use the above as an illustration of the fact that the help we give to those who are underprivileged must be long term, not short term, help. It has become a habit in government to assume that government assistance, as well as person-to-person assistance, given to the so-called backward nations, can accomplish marvels in a couple of years and that then responsibility ceases. The history of the American Frontier shows that even Americans who prided themselves on being up-to-date resisted in almost every instance the assistance of doctors who were ahead of their times. If Americans had to have the value of surgery shown to them again and again before they were willing to accept it, it should not surprise us that we must have more long term projects to help the people of distant countries—especially of Asia and Africa.

Since the war between Vietminh and Viet Nam, Dr. Thomas Dooley has done an extraordinary piece of work in his two year projects.* Dr. Dooley is a rock-breaker, the kind of pioneer that is needed everywhere. He breaks the rocks of prejudice against modern medicine and shows the people what modern medicine can do for them. But rock crushing is not enough. In a two-year term of service not even a permanent foundation can be laid, let alone a structure built which will be of permanent value.

I am reminded of Stilwell's campaign in 1943-44. We came down through the wild Naga Hills of northwest Burma and the bulldozers pushed down in a short time huge areas of impenetrable forests. Temporary structures were built, as, for example, the 1500 bed evacuation hospital at Shinbwiyang. That hospital had everything; but with the end of the war, all the Americans went home, and they tell me that today you cannot even locate the site of many of the installations—the jungle has completely taken over again. Similarly, in the case of Dr. Schweitzer, who has been working for a long time in Lambarene; his work is not yet complete and he can ill be spared. I have spent years here and am still not convinced that this area will not "return to jungle" unless American-Burmese cooperation continues during the years to come.

When Americans organize practical assistance to help the medically underprivileged, I am convinced that it should be,

* Dr. Dooley is largely responsible for the creation of MEDICO, originally a division of the International Rescue Committee established to give medical, scientific, and educational assistance to areas of need abroad by providing and supporting properly equipped medical teams to set up small clinics and train indigenous personnel with the objectives of turning the operation of the clinic over to the host government within a two year period when possible.—Ed.

at first, only on a person-to-person basis and without government funds. Burma, for example, will not accept American Government financial gifts. But the Burmese accept the idea of person-to-person assistance, and the Government allows them to accept such financial gifts if given privately and without political strings attached. Second, on the basis of my work in Namkham, which is an overgrown village, and of Dr. Dooley's work in the village centers of Laos, I am convinced that all private American help to foreign countries should go to the villages. The governments themselves will work out from the cities, and eventually the two services will supplement each other. Third, all American assistance should be determined by the practical needs of the countries. Specialists in some narrow specialized fields of medicine will find little that they can do in village institutions. The need is for doctors of the general practitioner type, men willing to take any kind of case coming to them. The old joke of the medical practitioner, "I specialize on the skin and its contents," is not a joke in these areas. It is a literal necessity where many of a doctor's patients will come to him, ailing with from four to six major diseases at once.

During the years of colonial rule I organized many small hospitals on a private basis and without government funds. When I proved the value of these small, scattered institutions, the Government began to give them grants-in-aid. Now all these small institutions are financed and managed by the Government, while Namkham remains the center to which patients these small institutions cannot treat are sent for definitive treatment.

With the removal of the colonial yoke from these countries and the consequent change in the spirit of the people, there has been an increased appreciation of schools and hospitals and an increased problem of staffing them. You can take somebody who has just finished middle school and use him as a teacher in that same middle school without further training and get by with it temporarily. Hospitals are much more difficult. It is almost impossible to increase rapidly the number of colleges of medicine and train qualified doctors. It is much easier to train nurses if you are willing to accept for training inferior girls. But unless trained nurse-midwives are highly qualified and are of very good stock to begin with, they cannot be sent out into village areas on their own where there are no doctors to supervise their work. I am told that many nurse-midwives who qualified during the last year have been unable to secure jobs. This, of course, does not mean that Burma is saturated with nurses; Burma needs a hundred times as many nurses as are available now. It means that established institutions with sufficient funds to support them do not yet exist.

Since the beginning of our hospital work at Namkham, I have used nurses in as many functions as possible. As a doctor, I refused to do anything a nurse could be taught to do. Since nurses had to be used as interpreters anyway, I taught them how to take case histories, a procedure we still follow at Namkham. I also taught them to give hypodermic and intramuscular injections. Later I let them give intravenous injections—I myself was their first patient—and they became so expert that none of us doctors now dares to compete with a skilled nurse in giving an intravenous injection. We taught them to give anesthetics during the war, and not one of us here can compete with the girls the anesthetists trained at that time. I never sew up a wound now. After I have finished the critical part of the operation, my first assistant, a nurse, closes the wound under my supervision. In other words, nurses play a vital role in our institution—they multiply the doctor's hands.

Hospitals are much more costly than schools and yet the demand for nursing care and hospital care is increasing by leaps and bounds. We have a 250 bed hospital—or, more accurately, a 250 mat hospital since all our patients are on mats. A few days ago, when I went on duty for my afternoon consultations, I found the admission department of the hospital jammed with new patients who had come by bus, truck, and jeep, private cars and chartered vehicles of all sorts, some of them from places more than 300 miles distant.

I know many scientists are worrying about overpopulation, fearing that the world will never produce food enough for all. India is especially a worry because of its rapidly increasing population. I heard one scientist say that it was a pity that the greatly improved medical facilities in India kept so many people from dying. It was his thesis that it would be better to permit famine, cholera, smallpox, and other epidemics and loathsome diseases to continue to keep the population at a low level so that sufficient feed could be grown for them. This seems to me an immoral point of view. There are other ways to control overpopulation, and food supply, as the United States has so ably demonstrated during the past twenty years, can be enormously increased. It is cruel to recommend that others suffer things which we ourselves will not tolerate; that others uselessly die by the millions while we ourselves are extending in an astounding way the longevity of the American people. We need the people of Asia and Africa in order to make a world in which it is fit to live; and we can help them.

In Burma one of our biggest medical problems is sterility. Burma is the only underpopulated country in the Far East, and the people of Burma feel exactly like the Jews of the Bible with regard to sterility. With one-child sterility, however, we apparently have obtained cures in about three-fifths of the cases, and women come to us from all over the northern half of Burma because friends of theirs were cured of the same type of sterility. There are many children in Namkham who are living proof of our cure of primary sterility, but it is a special feather in my cap that we now have in training one nurse and have already graduated another nurse whose mothers we cured of primary sterility by operation. Both these girls took up nursing as a profession because their mothers had told them that they existed only because of operations performed here.

During the years we have had many cases of extra-uterine pregnancy, but they were all ruptured when they arrived because, until recently, women did not come to us for even severe pain. They came only when the pain was excruciating and they felt a sudden rapid loss of strength. In obstetrics the picture is also changing. Women are coming to us, sometimes two months in advance. Among these we have had to perform an astonishing number of Caesarean sections— astonishing for us, that is. These Caesarean sections were not only for placenta previa, which we almost never saw until recently since the women died at home, but for very markedly contracted pelves. This is an entirely new development among our people and is undoubtedly the result of malnutrition during the Japanese occupation. In the prewar years we almost never saw a contracted pelvis, but now they are extremely common. I have had two Caesarean sections in a day more than once, and during the last three months we have had to screen off a section of the Women's Surgical Ward for the children born by Caesarean. There is not room enough in our maternity building to take care of all these cases since that building is continuously crowded by ordinary complicated and uncomplicated cases. How we will continue to take care of obstetrical and pediatric patients at all I do not know. I think this example will show that we are reaping altogether too rapidly, for our own and our patients' welfare, the fruits of seed sown many years before the war. We used to have to urge patients to care for themselves and come early. Now we do not know how to handle them properly in the numbers in which they are coming. If all the really sick people of this one valley came to us for treatment—they go, if possible, to government hospitals and dispensaries when they are not too badly off— we would be swamped and have no room for the thousands who come from hundreds of miles away. This proves, I think, my thesis that long term projects, even though conducted by a series of "short-term men," is essential if our service to neglected humanity is to be real and not just a flash in the pan.

I doubt if any American doctor would believe that some of the emaciated children and infants we have seen recently could live for a day, let alone exist long enough for our medicines to take effect. I have never before seen such emaciation, nor such advanced cases of rickets, nor so many children with only 10-15 per cent of hemoglobin on account of dysentery, malaria, or avitaminosis. And yet these children live. We have had a large run of adult patients with the same very low percentage of hemoglobin, but with the adult patients we are able to build up the hemoglobin with intravenous injections of iron, liver extract, Vitamin B12 and folic acid. We cannot use intravenous injections for babies, and yet they not only live but we have discharged many of these skeletons quite plump and well when their parents consented to remain here long enough for us to succeed. All this means an extraordinary increase in expenditure on costly drugs, but nothing worth while is cheap.

Our doctors have been astounded at the number of patients with less than 25 per cent of hemoglobin who have lived following major operations. This brings up a matter which has hurt me ever since I first came to Namkham: the fact that in these less developed areas of the world we cannot get donors for transfusions or organize a blood bank.

I understand that the Rangoon General Hospital now has a blood bank; but if so, it is a result of continuous propaganda on the part of the Government. Besides, the Burmese of the plains average 80 per cent of hemoglobin. Up in our country, which is the homeland of plasmodium falciparum and entamoeba histolytica and where approximately 90 per cent of all our patients have hookworm, we look upon 60 per cent of hemoglobin as being normal. One cannot really blame people like this when they refuse to give transfusions and even refuse to have a few cc's of blood removed for cross-matching. When possible we try to persuade the patient to remain with us long enough so that medical treatment will bring his blood up to at least 45 per cent before an operation is performed. This is extremely difficult to do, even with elective surgery, because 90 per cent or more of our patients are so poor that they cannot afford the time here in the hospital. Furthermore, many of the operations are emergencies. Yet our mortality rate remains low.

Before the war it seemed stupid to me to teach nurses about gallstone because we practically never found a case; and cholecystitis was almost unheard of. This year cholelithiasis, cholecystitis, hydrops, and empyema of the gallbladder have come in numbers that practically amount to an epidemic. There was one severe epidemic of typhoid that I remember before the war. We lost one nurse from a typhoid perforation which occurred while I was away. The typhoid we had in those days was comparatively mild. The last two years it has been extremely severe, and one entire family of five came in with typhoid, two of the children already perforated. We saved one but not the other.

I do very little surgery myself if the other doctors are trained in that branch of surgery, because I want them to obtain all the experience that they can. Usually I do only the obstetrical surgery which they have not yet begun to study. But when they open a belly that is so messed up that they cannot figure out what to do next, they send for me to use my sense of touch with which their own can still not compare. I use that sense of touch in separating the organs until we reach the point where they are familiar with the pathology that still needs to be handled; and then I leave them to finish the operation. Occasionally patients who have known me for years will permit only me to operate on them.

The good doctors of countries like Burma will blossom forth into real surgeons in their own right. They spend every spare minute studying up their cases in all the latest surgical textbooks and reading from cover to cover every medical magazine that comes to us. Now I frequently call my assistants in as consultants. Last year a Palong girl, 16 years old, was admitted with a bony ankylosis of both elbows in extension and with osteomyelitis of the right radius, all following an attack of smallpox when she was four years old. One of my doctors operated on the left elbow first, doing an arthroplasty which was so successful that he later operated on the right elbow. The girl left the hospital in October with both elbows moving freely without pain. I personally have never been able to do a successful arthroplasty.

On January 9, last year, a nine-year-old Chinese boy had his trousers catch fire. He was brought here the next morning with deep burns of both legs reaching up to the waist line. I had learned during the last few days of the war that none of us doctors could handle a burn case as successfully as our top nurse, Naomi, who has been frequently mentioned in my books. Naomi is much more gentle and patient than I. We doctors took care of the shock and the medicinal treatment given, and Naomi took care of the burns, debriding where necessary and using pressure bandages. As soon as a patch of healthy granulations appeared Naomi herself pinch-grafted the areas, doing all the painful dressings. As late as June we were still using plasma substitutes and anti-biotics. The case was not uncomplicated. The boy acquired malaria during his stay in the hospital. He was not discharged until the 14th of August during which time we had spent several thousands of dollars in his treatment. Naomi was so pleased with her results that she made me travel all the way up to his ward to take a look at him before he was discharged. I have never seen such a perfect result. Thousands of pinch-grafts, done at exactly the right time—she chose the times, I did not—had resulted in an extraordinary pair of legs. There was no limitation of movement either of flexion or of extension. Nurses can be used to thus increase the help which the doctors give.

I mention these individual cases to emphasize the fact that among the medically underprivileged of Asia and Africa one finds a great deal more than tropical diseases. They have these, but they have also the diseases common in America.

If we had millions of dollars to spend, the amount could very well be spent in this area alone. The first thing that we would do, if consent of the Government could be obtained, would be to import some ten American specialists to use Namkham as a base. The line of attack which we follow in our hospital work is the opposite of that followed by all governments. Whatever a government does must, of necessity, begin in the capital, then branch out into larger cities, then the towns and finally, at long last, it reaches the villages and the farmers. This is the only way a government can act. But, in the Orient at least, the village is the strategic unit, and it is among these common people that the dissatisfactions that respond to Communism appear. With us Namkham is just a village. We began with the village, and gradually our influence spread until people from the cities began to come to us. Since this village of ours is right on a Communist border, I very sincerely believe in our hospital's mission for the people of Burma and so do all these precious staff nurses that we have been selecting so carefully for so many years. They have stood by me and the hospital through thick and thin. I believe it would be a tragedy for the people of Burma, north of Mandalay at least, if anything destroys this hospital work. My one earnest hope is that when I die I can leave it in such a prosperous condition that nothing will destroy the private enterprise and the nonsectarian, non-profit, charitable nature of this institution.

There are still in Burma three very backward areas in which no proper medical work is being done: the first of these is the Wa States just southeast of us which is ruled partly by China and partly by Burma; the second is the "Triangle," the mountainous area between the two rivers which form the Irrawaddy, in the Kachin State to the northwest; and the third is the Naga Hills area lying between us and Nehru's Assam. The Nagas are ruled on the west by India and on the east by Burma. Both the Nagas and the Was are still head-hunters and the Kachins in the "Triangle," I am told, still offer human sacrifice to their evil spirits. Nurses of ours have served in the Wa States and in Kokang, a Chinese state just north of the Was, which belongs to Burma. In order to entice nurses to work either in the Wa States or the Kokang, the Government pays them a salary fabulously large for Burma. One of our nurse graduates makes periodic trips into the "Triangle."

In cities like Rangoon the Government has now developed doctors of very considerable skill, and there is an intensive program of sending the graduates of the medical college abroad for further study. In addition, the Government has brought in many specialists from the United Nations, from the United States and other countries, to teach their specialties in Burma. So, perhaps, in certain parts of Burma which are well supplied with a few first-class institutions, the people of Burma are not all underprivileged medically. Yet those areas are still very small. But although they may not be absolutely underprivileged now, time will not stand still. Medical science has not lost the impetus which began some 70 years ago with the development of aseptic surgery. The increase of knowledge in all the medical sciences has developed with a speed unknown to previous history. Something must be done to see that that increase of knowledge is given to our friends in Asia and Africa.

Do not believe that the people of Asia and Africa are ignorant of the developments in medical science. They read about them and they want them for themselves. If we do not help them to obtain these improvements, we will lose some of our best friends.

THE CHILDREN

By SPURGEON M. KEENY

> The children of Asia, starving, under-
> nourished, ill, improperly cared for,
> are "neighbors" to Spurgeon Keeny.

SPURGEON M. KEENY has since the last war devoted himself to relief programs in various parts of the world. A graduate of Gettysburg College, where he was elected to Phi Beta Kappa and from which he also received an M.A., he pursued further study in English at the University of Chicago and at Harvard and subsequently received the B.A. and M.A. in English literature at Oxford.

Mr. Keeny served in Russia from 1922 to 1924, under Herbert Hoover, in the American Relief Administration. Thereafter for eighteen years he served with the National Council of YMCA's, and from 1935 to 1942 was the executive secretary of the Council's Public Affairs Committee, during the last year also serving as a consultant with the Office of Price Administration.

In 1943 the State Department called Mr. Keeny into duty as coordinator of supply requirements for Civilian Relief. The next year he served as consultant to the combined US-British Chiefs of Staff. Among his duties was assistance in establishing standards for civilian relief after the Allied invasion of Italy, and serving as a member of the UNRRA Headquarters Staff.

In 1947 Mr. Keeny became chief of the UNRRA Mission in Italy and soon was made chief of the International Refugee Organization Mission. From 1948 to 1950 he was chief of the European Supply Office of UNICEF in Paris, and since that time he has served as director of the Asia Region of this organization.

Mr. Keeny is author of *Half the World's Children* and of articles in the *Atlantic Monthly,* the British *Lancet,* and many other periodicals. He has been decorated by the Italian Government and the Knights of Malta.

The Children

"I stopped for a moment, in my lonely way under the starlight, and saw spread before me the darkened earth surrounding with her arms countless homes furnished with cradles and beds, mothers' hearts and evening lamps, and young lives glad with a gladness that knows nothing of its value for the world."—Rabindranath Tagore

*T*HE INVITATION to write this chapter reaches me in Bangkok, almost exactly on the other side of the world from the United States. Just outside my office window, on the Chao Phya River, hundreds of small boats hurry to and fro as the people of the city work to earn their rice. Nearer, by a hydrant in the compound, half a dozen naked children are happily pouring water on themselves in the approved manner for Thais bathing. It is a good place to ask myself how I got into work for children and what I am working for.

As I look back, it all started on the Pennsylvania farm where I was born. My grandfather, who was a Dunkard, and his seven children, took it for granted that we should

help a sick neighbor harvest his wheat or build a new barn
when lightning had burned the old one. My first contacts
with outsiders were with the friendly tramps who regularly
slept in our barn—of course, after leaving their matches at
the house.

It was natural then, when I ventured out into the world,
that I should grow as the twig had been bent. During and
after World War I, I worked with the YMCA helping prisoners of war and refugees return to their homes and start
life over again. On these errands I found myself in turn in
Mesopotamia, Siberia, Esthonia, Poland, Czechoslovakia,
and Soviet Russia, where I helped fight the famine that
killed millions in the early 20's.

Between wars I kept on with the YMCA in the United
States, enlisting the aid of people of good will to help our
American boys from poorer homes get a better start in life.

During World War II I worked in the State Department,
helping plan what could be done for the civilian populations
if and when the Allies again could set foot on the continent
of Europe. Then followed several years when I had to put
some of these plans into effect in helping Italy out of the
ruins of war. There, as chief of the United Nations Relief
and Rehabilitation Administration mission I saw the possibilities—and difficulties—of intergovernmental aid. There
also I had reinforced the conviction I had reached in Russia
that the greatest sufferers after a war are the children. I
determined, if possible, to give the rest of my life to them.
The chance came through the United Nations Children's
Fund (UNICEF); ten years ago I found myself assigned as
Director for Asia. I am still here.

There was no lack of opportunity. Of the nine hundred
million children in the world, more than half are in Asia.
Communist China has not accepted UN aid, but there remained something over two hundred and fifty million chil-

dren we could serve. But what could we do with only five or six million dollars a year?

The first thing to do was to learn how the people really live. Tourists who visit Asia see mostly its crowded cities, but more than four out of five people live in the country, usually in small villages. Let me introduce you to a typical family.

Mr. and Mrs.. Darnchoomporn, and their two children, Tonolai, aged five, and Boonchan, nine, live in the province of Prachinburi, in northeast Thailand. They are rice farmers with about ten acres of land. This is a lot for Thailand, but the land is not very good in that province. The harvest every year amounts to about six bullock carts of rice—just enough for the family to eat. The value of their crop is about one hundred and fifty dollars. In the off-season the husband cuts wood for another twenty-five dollars. His wife raises a few chickens, but the family do not eat the eggs—they grow more chickens, which they sell: that brings in another twenty-five dollars. They grow a few vegetables and have a couple of fruit trees, which bring in just about enough to offset their taxes and their gifts to the temple. Altogether, they have the equivalent of about two hundred dollars a year for four people.

The Darnchoomporn family may have only a dollar a week each but they are important people: they are the average family of Asia. To accept and understand the starkly simple fact that the average person in Asia lives on a dollar a week is one of the hardest things we Americans have to learn. Until we have learned it, we cannot give much useful advice.

Fortunately, UNICEF was starting to work at the beginning of a new era in medicine. DDT was available to stop the transmission of malaria, and numerous new drugs to cure it quickly. Penicillin would cure yaws, many types of pneu-

monia, and other diseases as well. The sulpha drugs were
ready to fight intestinal diseases. Other antibiotics were
available for that scourge of Asia, the eye disease of trachoma. Bacillus Calmette-Guerin (BCG) vaccine would
help prevent tuberculosis, and new drugs would help cure
it. Except for BCG, none of these were known twenty years
before and some not even ten.

The practical application of new mechanical inventions
in the last century often took decades—sometimes almost a
century. Asia could not wait so long. A way had to be
found to speed up the process.

In the field of health that way was found in a partnership
of governments, the World Health Organization (WHO),
and UNICEF. WHO aided the doctors in each country to
make the plans; UNICEF agreed to supply free the drugs
that had to be imported. The two organizations went together like ham and eggs.

We were painfully aware that, as the UN Bill of Human
Rights proclaims, good health is the right of every child; we
also knew that prevention is better than cure. But the hard
facts were that, in Asia at least, one child in five died in the
first year and another one in the next five years. Also, there
were very few doctors—and those mostly in the cities. In the
country, it is not uncommon to find one hundred thousand
people with a single doctor—and sometimes with none.

Under these circumstances we had to start with the things
that *must* be done. One of them was birth: babies don't wait
until there are doctors to deliver them. Every year at least
twenty five million new babies are born in Asia, excluding
China. UNICEF began by helping train midwives and to
get them out into the villages. In the first ten years it has
helped governments establish more than ten thousand
mother-and-child centers. Even then, more than three-
quarters of the babies are being delivered by traditional

birth attendants—older women of the village whose mothers and grandmothers had done the same thing.

These birth attendants have a lot of practical knowledge and they are usually well thought of in the village. And for good reasons: they not only deliver the baby, but they cook meals for the father, look after the other children, and feed the buffalo and chickens as well. For their services they get on the average about two dollars for a boy baby and one for a girl.

One thing they don't know about is germs. They have never seen any, and no one has told them. And so, with dirty hands, they often poison the mother while they are trying to help. In one country, they believe firmly that the way to insure that a new-born baby will love its father is to clap onto the newly cut cord a piece of papa's clothing— usually a shirt waiting to be washed. The result is often lockjaw and death.

The superstitions are many, but most of them are harmless. In parts of Pakistan it is thought that baby's entry into the world will be easier if everything is open. So the careful midwife will open all the doors, locked chests, and every drawer in the house. If these practices are harmless and give confidence, they are not interfered with. The important thing is to change the few superstitions that really do harm.

The training of these birth attendants goes on apace. Up to now, some thirty thousand have been given simple instructions, mostly on cleanliness. Each is given, on "graduation," a shiny new midwife's bag on condition that she reports to the health center all pregnancies in her village and especially all cases that threaten to be abnormal. From being a potential threat to life, she is thus becoming an important link in the chain of health services to the village.

Birth is only the first of the dangers baby must face. Asia is full of diseases that the United States has forgotten—and

of those we never knew. True, the classic epidemics of smallpox, plague, and cholera are on the wane (although there
are 75 cases of cholera in Bangkok this week); but there
are plenty more people with other diseases that crowd the
hospitals and health centers, where they do, and must, get
first attention. So long as there are sick babies waiting, the
doctor and the nurse can't stop their work to hold a well-
baby clinic. Some of the diseases we still don't know how to
eradicate or even control, but there are five that can be
stamped at costs that even Asia can afford. These are malaria,
tuberculosis, yaws (a form of ulcer that occurs only in the
tropics), trachoma, and leprosy. These five UNICEF determined to help attack because all of them are especially
the enemies of children.

The worst enemy of all is malaria, the greatest killer in
Asia. The conquest of this single disease can reduce the
death rate in children by as much as one half in as little as
ten years or even less. More than half a billion people in
Asia are constantly threatened by the disease, three hundred
million of them seriously. Thanks to a joint effort by the
United States Government, the World Health Organization,
and UNICEF, almost half of all these people are being pro-
tected by 1960. By 1965, most of Asia's malaria will be gone.

The second killer is tuberculosis. This enemy is more stub-
born, and we must look for at least twenty-five years of
bitter fighting before it comes under control. As one part of
UNICEF's effort against this disease, we have helped the
governments test more than 200 million children and vac-
cinate those who needed it. The number tested is four times
all the children in the United States.

The best news of progress is against the third enemy, especially of children—yaws. Here the job in Asia was to cure
about 15 million cases, three-fourths of them in Indonesia.

A start was made only 10 years ago; today more than half the job has been done. A single shot of penicillin costing about five cents cures a child.

The fourth enemy is trachoma, of which there are at least 100 million cases in Asia. This disease is the largest single cause of blindness, but the fight against it has only begun with the new antibiotics. But we know it can be done: the million children cured in Taiwan alone are the proof.

The fifth battle is against leprosy, which has ceased to be a dread incurable scourge and is now only one more communicable disease that can be cured with several years' regular treatment. The hardest part is to find the patients, who are still afraid that they will be taken from their families and locked up in leprosaria. They are being treated now in their own homes. The drugs to cure a case cost about a dollar. We are only at the very beginning of this task, with less than one hundred thousand cases being treated with UNICEF aid out of at least 3 million. But the work is gathering speed. It must: we cannot afford to wait; for most leprosy is caught in childhood. If detected early, it can be cured within a year and often within six months.

When this underbrush has been cut away, the building of permanent rural health programs can begin. In another ten years the 10 thousand health centers will have doubled, more staff will have been trained, who will do much better work than they do now.

All our efforts to help bring health to Asia, however, will come to nothing if the children don't have enough to eat— and they don't. The average child in India eats only about half as much as one in the United States—and food of poorer quality. The greatest single enemy of the child in Asia is hunger. There are small gains each year, but people are still eating less than they did before World War II. The United

188 Spurgeon M. Keeny

States has made its surplus of milk powder (some three hundred thousand tons a year) available free, and Asia has received more than half of the total. Here UNICEF has helped, but is playing a minor role as the Protestant and Roman Catholic organizations (and CARE) have organized their extensive relief services. The distribution is coordinated; the only thing wrong is that there ought to be more of it.

In the long run, however, Asia must produce its own food. The UN Food and Agriculture Organization has primary responsibility in the conservation of milk and of the increased production of other high-protein foods. With UNICEF assistance Bombay, for example, will soon have milk enough for nearly two-thirds of its people—and for nearly all its children. UNICEF buys the imported machinery and gets paid back (with interest) in milk which goes free or subsidized to the poorer children of the city.

Thus have I spent the last ten years. I've traveled some 700,000 miles and visited most of the countries in Asia, from Afghanistan to Japan, on the average twenty times, getting to know the village life. Much of it is still to me what William James said the world must be to a young baby: "a great, booming confusion." But, out of these thousands of contacts with people, I feel sure of at least a few things:

1. The achievements I have mentioned are but a tiny fraction of what is being done around the world by many agencies, public and private.
2. Nearly every government in the world is helping in this mutual aid. The United States is doing more than any other government but, with its vast resources, not so much as it should do.
3. The foundation for the present expansion of work for children has been laid by the Christian churches. What

is now being done largely by governments is an extension of the same spirit of good will and desire to share.

4. We must deal with all peoples as equals. Colonialism is gone but the colonial mind is still too much with us— and not only in the countries that have the most colonies.

5. In particular, we whites must free ourselves from feelings of superiority because we are white. Asia has more than a billion people who are not white nor do they wish to be.

6. While guarding against undue nationalism ourselves, we must be patient with it in new countries. Freedom is a heady drink.

7. Whatever their color or creed, we who work for the children of the world must like people for themselves. We must learn their languages and respect their customs as we want ours respected.

8. We must work through the people of a country; the leaders must be local leaders.

9. We must not be greedy for gratitude for our gifts. The people most fluent with their thanks are often professional beggars.

10. We must lay our plans for mutual aid carefully but must not be satisfied forever with little experiments. The way to success is to do more each year of what needs to be done.

Atomic power and rocketry have given enormous impetus to our imagination—often in harmful directions when they have multiplied our fears. I often share Earl Attlee's wish that we should leave the moon alone and get busy making this planet a better one for all people to live on. If we can take our eyes off the moon occasionally, I think there is a good chance of realizing the hope that Arnold Toynbee expressed when he said that our century will probably be remembered, not for its two world wars, but as the period in which, for the first time, the idea of mutual aid among the nations to raise the standard of living everywhere became accepted.

THE

ILLITERATE

By FRANK C. LAUBACH

> Those who never learned to read or write, the native tribes with no written language, the illiterates in some 90 countries, are "neighbors" to Frank Laubach.

FRANK C. LAUBACH, world-famed pioneer in the literacy movement, is responsible for millions of people throughout the world learning to read and write. Born in Pennsylvania in 1884, Dr. Laubach studied at Perkiomen Seminary, Princeton University, and Union Theological Seminary; he received his Ph.D. at Columbia University.

Dr. Laubach's interest in literacy teaching began some thirty years ago when he was a missionary in the Philippines among the Moro who spoke a primitive language which had never been put into writing. Here he began the development of the Laubach literacy method through which he has helped to fight illiteracy in 91 countries.

Until retirement in 1954, Dr. Laubach worked under the sponsorship of the National Council of Churches of Christ in the USA. As honorary president of World Literacy, Inc., with headquarters in New York, he is continuing to lead in the world's battle against illiteracy with teams of experts, providing technical assistance in literacy work to governments of countries in which from 75 to 90 per cent of the adults cannot read or write.

Dr. Laubach has been a consultant to UN agencies and to many governments. He holds honorary degrees from Syracuse, Princeton, Temple, and Columbia Universities, and from Wooster, Lafayette, and Muskingum Colleges.

Few men are so widely travelled as Dr. Laubach, and few are greeted with such genuine affection wherever they go. In dozens of countries, people know him as "Bapa," which means father. Tribes of the Belgian Congo gave him the title of "Okombekombe" or "mender of old baskets" because he taught older people to read and write. In Cuba he is called the "Man with the Flaming Heart."

Among the books Dr. Laubach has written are *The Silent Billion Speak* and *Wake Up or Blow Up.*

The Illiterate

*I*N JESUS' familiar parable, the good Samaritan was an alien, a foreigner despised by the Jews. Through this story Jesus made clear that our duty to help those in need extends to any man who has "fallen among robbers and been left half-dead" even if he belongs to an alien race.

More than half the people of the world have fallen among thieves, who have robbed them and stripped them and left them half-dead. They are the illiterate people, across southern Asia, all over Africa, and over nearly all of Latin America. They are the victims of educated robbers because they cannot help themselves. And to us Jesus says, as emphatically as he said to the lawyer, "You must help those victims."

The United Nations has published a map showing the areas where people are hungry, live in mud huts, are without money or without even the comforts of life, and where they are shot full of disease. The United Nations has published another map, showing where people are illiterate. The two maps are exactly the same because illiteracy makes people the victims of hunger, poverty and exploitation. Where people are illiterate they are unable to protect themselves from robbers or from diseases, or from the insects that kill their plants and their animals. Their agriculture is so primitive that they cannot produce as much as they consume.

Most people are shocked when they learn for the first time that these hungry people are getting hungrier, that there are more people on the verge of starvation today than there were 50 years ago. We who are educated are getting richer. But those who are illiterate are getting hungrier. This widening chasm between the educated people who have, and the illiterate people who have not, is the most dangerous fact in the world today. Communism arose from the desperation of the have-nots and is still making tremendous inroads among them. If all the Communists in the world died tomorrow, the terrible wrong which produced Communism would still be here. So this is our concern; it is our business whether we are Christians trying to help our fellow men, or whether we are concerned about our own country. We have a terrible mandate to reach these hungry illiterates, and we must do it soon. Time is running out. James Michener printed the statement that we are losing a hundred million of the hungry illiterate people of Asia and Africa to Communism every year. At that rate we shall have passed the point of no return in from 5 to 10 years.

But can we reach these illiterates soon enough? Yes, if we make an all-out effort far greater than we have made up to this time. In all 97 countries in which I have worked, I have found them eager to learn to read and write. They know they are hungry because they are ignorant. And they want to come up out of their hunger and their ignorance more than anything else in the world. Fortunately also these 97 governments are now eager to make their people literate.

This was not true 40 years ago. At that time the educated people in the illiterate areas were exploiting the illiterates, taking advantage of cheap labor, feeding them just enough to keep them alive. Many educated people believed that if these illiterates learned to read, they would be unwilling to work. At that time nobody, except a few of the missionaries who strongly emphasized reading the Bible, cared whether the people could read or not. It was among these missionaries that the modern movement for teaching illiterates began. But today the situation is completely changed. Communist agitators have infiltrated among the ignorant multitudes of Asia and Africa and Latin America, inciting them to overthrow their governments. And this has the governments and educated people thoroughly alarmed. Some of them are good, some of them are bad, but they are all alike in one respect. They are terrified at the rising rebelliousness of their own illiterate masses, and are eager to satisfy their demands. The doors are wide open to missionaries who are experts in the technique of teaching illiterates—especially by the Each-One-Teach-One Method—and to those who can write simply and attractively the things which these illiterates demand to help them help themselves.

Literacy is the service most open to the Christian Church today around the whole underprivileged world. It can become the Church's most powerful instrument for evangelism.

I first discovered this for myself among the Mohammedan Moros of the Philippine Islands. They were violently prejudiced against the Gospel, just as the Arab Moslems now are. For 15 years we made attempts to start religious services, but not a single Mohammedan would come. Then we began teaching them to read, because we found that they were eager to learn. Now came the stunning surprise. Nobody at all would come to our religious services, but hundreds and later even thousands came to learn to read. We were thronged and overwhelmed. We had 400 volunteer teachers who brought a thousand names a month of people whom they had taught to read.

Fortunately the Maranaw language was one of the easiest in the world to teach. It had only 16 sounds, one letter for a sound; and when the people knew these sounds they could pronounce every word in their language. Almost everybody was reading slowly but understandingly within three days to a week after they began to study.

Our second discovery was that when lessons are very easy to learn and easy to teach, the poor people liked to teach one another at home if we provided them with cheap little four-page primers. Illiterate people have no money and never expect pay from one another. They help each other build their houses and plant their crops. And so they were glad to teach each other without receiving any remuneration.

Our next discovery was that everybody we taught became our friend. When we first reached Lanao, we had only one Mohammedan friend, and he was a murderer who had been saved from the gallows by an American lieutenant. He taught us to speak the Maranaw language. It was not safe for us to venture out of the military camp without soldier escort. But within a year after beginning literacy work everybody in the province had become our friend. The Moslems began to come to our Sunday religious services— even the highest chiefs in the province. When young Moros joined our Church, there was no opposition even from the priests. Direct preaching had utterly failed for fifteen years. But literacy had won the entire province over to our friendship and had begun to make some of them Christian within one year.

News of this so-called "Miracle of Lanao" spread over the rest of the Philippine Islands. The Secretary of the National

Christian Council and the Superintendent of the public schools asked me to make lessons in other languages, like those we had made for the Maranaw Moros. In about three years we had lessons in 20 Philippine dialects.

Letters began to come from other parts of the world where missionaries felt the need of literacy and wanted to know about our methods. At this time a book by Dr. Daniel Fleming called *The Marks of a World Christian* fell into my hands. It contained the startling news that two-thirds of the world was still illiterate. We made a large map of the world with the Philippine Islands in the center, and on this map we pinned a red silk thread stretching from every country that wrote to us, down to our province. Soon we had a wheel of silk threads, five hundred of them, from every continent and from almost every underprivileged country. The Moros gazed at this map with great delight, and said, "We are going to show the whole world how to become literate."

In 1935 when we took our furlough, we came back to America by way of Singapore, Ceylon, India, Egypt, Palestine and Turkey, trying our Moro method in those countries. We found the alphabets of India and of Egypt far harder than those of the Philippine Islands. But the passion to help these illiterate people was now coursing in our veins. For the past 25 years we have accepted invitations to work with missionaries and governments in Asia, Africa, Latin America, and the islands of the Pacific.

Our great interest was in showing the churches how to utilize literacy to win friends and to lead them to Christ. Let us take the Methodist Mission in Wembo Nyama in the heart of the Congo as an example. First, we worked with missionaries and native Christians in preparing a ten-page primer in the Otetela language. Then we spent several days training every member of the church to teach these lessons. Each member had to teach Lesson One perfectly. We told them how to treat illiterates to make them happy. "Never scold, never frown, never look disappointed, never say, 'No,' never ask a question which the illiterate cannot answer. Look pleased and surprised, and give him a great deal of praise. Don't talk much. Say only what is necessary. If you do it right you will give him the greatest hour of his life. At the end of the lesson, tell him why you are teaching him. Say to him: 'We Christians are teaching you because we learned this from Jesus. He loved people more than anybody in the world. He spent every minute of his day helping people. He went down the road looking for people in trouble. If they were hungry he fed them. If they were sick he healed them. If they were lame he made them walk. If they were blind he opened their eyes. You and all of your village are blind to the secrets that the educated people have in books. That is the reason you are hungry. But Jesus sent us here to open your eyes, and now you and your children will know those secrets, and you will never be the same. If you let Jesus into your life as we do, it is wonderful what he will do for you.' " At the end of each lesson we had a witness story about Jesus and his wonderful compassion. The one thing that people in the world cannot resist is the tremendous love of Jesus.

After all of the members had been taught to teach others, they went to the adjoining village and each selected some illiterate to teach. Then every day, in the big yard surrounding the church, there were hunderds of little groups of two, each one teaching one. One man walked 200 miles because he heard that there was an "injection for ignorance." Miss Eye, the nurse, laughed until the tears ran down her cheeks and said, "There is a man near here who can give you that injection." She brought him over to the group where we were training the teachers, and told us what he wanted; so we gave him his first "injection" in front of the class of teachers. When he found how easy it was to learn, he laughed and cried and jumped and shouted, all at once. He had gone crazy with joy. And the class had to break up till he had got over his hysteria. This is the way the illiterates all over the world feel when they begin to learn to read. It is like getting out of Hell into Heaven.

In about ten days we had taught the first Primer to 200 illiterates. Then we had a graduation ceremony. The District Director of Education, a Roman Catholic, came to distribute the diplomas. Each member of the church who was teaching brought his pupil forward. The teacher received a certificate of Christian service, and the student received a diploma which said, "This student has finished the Primer and is now ready to study *The Story of Jesus.*" *The Story of Jesus* is a very, very simple version of the four Gospels, so simple that it can be read easily after the student finishes the Primer. Here is the first chapter; containing ten new words not found in the Primer, each word repeated five times to help the memory:

> This is the story of Jesus.
> This is the story of Mary.
> This is the story of the angel.
> The angel said to Mary, Mary, you will be a mother.
> The angel said to Mary, Mary, you will have a child.
> Mary said to the angel,
> I have no husband. I cannot be a mother.
> Mary said to the angel,
> I have no husband. I cannot have a child.
> The angel said to Mary,
> You have no husband but you can be a mother.
> You have no husband but you can have a child.
> God will give you a child; God will give you Jesus.
> Mary sang: I will be a mother.
> Mary sang: I will have a child.
> Mary sang: God will give me a child.

Mary sang: God will give me Jesus.
Mary sang and sang and sang and sang.
This is the story of Mary.
This is the story of the angel.
This is the story of Jesus.

There are 100 stories like this, covering the life of Jesus until the day of his ascension. This book is now in print in 80 languages, and is being translated for publication in many more. When the student has finished *The Story of Jesus,* he is able to read the four Gospels in his own language, but he is not able to read the Letters of the New Testament. So we have translated the Letters into very, very simple English, with very short sentences. For example, the first sentence in Romans in the Authorized Version is 120 words long. We have divided it into 13 different sentences. Thus we use literacy to enable the student to read the Bible.

In the past twelve years, as governments have grown increasingly worried about their hungry illiterates, they have been asking our literacy team to help them. They do not have enough money, or teachers, or buildings to teach the illiterates in the ordinary way. Their only hope is to make lessons which can be taught in the Each-One-Teach-One way. We have helped 75 different governments to prepare such lessons. In 1953 we were invited by the United States Government to join the Point Four Program in India and make literacy lessons for the Community Development Program. The Government of India, and every other government wants, not the Bible, but "how-to-do-it books" showing the illiterates how to improve their economic health. So we prepared a graded textbook called *Anand the Wise Man,* which begins where the Primer ends.

The book is the story of an Indian farmer who learned to read. Every lesson in the book told him a secret that helped him and his family and his community. In one chap-

ter he learned that he was sickly because he ate the wrong
kind of food, too much carbohydrate and no protein, though
of course we did not use those big words. The book told him
what to eat. In another lesson he learned that he was starving because he starved his land. The villagers of India take
the cow dung, dry it in the sun and use it for fuel. They
have no other kind of fuel for cooking or to keep them warm.
So they constantly rob their land of its fertility. Anand
learned that he ought to have a compost pit, throw all of
his leaves and filth and cow dung into that pit, allow it to
decay for three months, then put it on the land for fertilizer.
"Feed the land and the land will feed you." So Anand fer-
tilized his land, and it gave him four times as much crop
without any more work. In another lesson Anand learned
that his seeds were very poor and that he could exchange
them for some wonderful high-yielding seeds at the Government Seed Office. So he got the good seeds and his crops
were three times as good as in the previous year. Then
Anand read that his little wooden plow, which went only
one inch under the ground, needed an iron point, so he went
to the Government and got an iron point which went three
inches under the ground, and struck soil that had never been
used before. Then his crops were three times as good again
—without any more work than he had done before. But
his little oxen could not pull the plow with an iron point,
so he read how to cross-breed them with the new splendid
cattle which were being imported from abroad.

When the Indians read what Anand did, they say, "If he
could do it, we can too." Thus literacy has become a powerful aid to community projects. When the expert goes to the
villages where they have read *Anand,* he does not tell them
what to do. He asks them what they want, and they tell
him, "Get us some of these new seeds; get us iron points
on our plows; help us cross-breed our poor little oxen; get

us nitrogen for our soil." The very things he came to help them with are the very things they ask him to do.

So literacy not only leads people to Christ, but also leads them up, out of their poverty and hunger and despair, to a new level of decent living. Indeed, it is the "sound barrier" beyond which illiterates can never go until they have learned to read and have access to the books and magazines and catalogues and instructions and blueprints which mark the vast difference between progressive, civilized people and the stagnant, hungry despair of the illiterate world.

THE PEASANT FARMER

By WALTER C. LOWDERMILK

Those unaware of methods of soil and
water conservation, who do not know
how to conserve and use their land,
the peasant farmers throughout the
world, are "neighbors" to Walter
Lowdermilk.

WALTER CLAY LOWDERMILK has been concerned with the problem of soil conservation here and abroad for many years. After graduating from Park College and the University of Arizona, he went to Oxford as a Rhodes scholar and then took a Ph.D. at the University of California. After working as a forest ranger and a timber acquisition officer, he volunteered for the AEF and was with the Engineers Corps in France; he later became research officer for the U. S. Forest Service in 1919. From 1922 to 1927 he was professor of Forestry at the University of Nanking in China, then returned to the States where he served with the California Forest Experimental Station. From 1933 he worked for the Soil Conservation Service of the Department of Agriculture, retiring in 1947 as assistant chief and chief of Research.

Dr. Lowdermilk has served and continues to serve as consultant to various foreign governments and UN organizations on matters of soil and water conservation and land development. He was chairman of the Committee on Land Erosion of the International Union of Geodesy and Geophysics from 1951 to 1954 and was an FAO visiting professor of agricultural engineering at The Technion in Haifa, Israel, from 1955 to 1957. He is also a Fellow of the American Geographic Society and the American Society of Foresters, a member of the International Society of Soil Scientists, the Pacific Science Association, the Washington Academy of Science, the Society of American Military Engineers, and the American Geophysical Union.

In addition to technical reports, abstracts, and articles Dr. Lowdermilk is the author of *Tracing Land Use Across Ancient Boundaries, Palestine—Land of Promise, Eleventh Commandment,* and *Contour Farming for the Bible Lands.*

The Peasant Farmer

IN THIS modern world with its spectacular advances in science and technology, in mass production, in rapid transportation and communication, peoples around the world are actually becoming close neighbors, according to the ancient Chinese proverb "All men within the four seas are brothers." The biblical command to "love thy neighbor as thyself," places on "have nations" a great responsibility to assist and to collaborate with lesser developed countries, in the mutual interests of both. It is increasingly necessary to be good neighbors if peace on earth and good will toward men are to prevail.

While these great sayings lift our hopes, we are brought down to earth in our attempts to apply these principles and commandments to actual conditions. Especially do we have a tremendous challenge when we recognize as our neighbors the peasant farmers who represent more than two-thirds of mankind. They stand at a critical stage in advance of civilization between subsistence and industrialized economies.

205

We cannot escape their problems by "passing by on the other side," even if we would. For the fate of these neighbors will influence our own fortune and future.

In mankind's social progress, it is not until the farmer grows more food and crops than he and his family need, that his neighbors are released for other tasks in the division of labor in the industrial and service super-structure of society. The United Nations report of the Food and Agriculture Organization reveals that 70 per cent of the 2.8 billion peoples of the world are occupied in farming. But of these only about 10 per cent produce more than they need and have purchasing power to buy for themselves other good and useful things.

The vast majority of those who till the soil are subsistence or peasant farmers. They grow little or no surplus above their immediate needs and have practically no purchasing power in these agrarian economies. They do not share in the good things of modern civilization. They are now stirring with hopes and demands. They are much more easily inflamed by hatred and by lure of looting, than informed how to make the most of lands, waters, and minerals to produce abundantly for their needs and for products which they exchange through the medium of money for what they cannot produce.

We can know neither our peasant neighbor nor his problems from afar. We must discover firsthand his difficulties in growing food by traditional practices. Too long the problems of peasant farming had been considered as unworthy of the attention of scholars of the past, who had little interest in production, or of divines of old who were more interested in heaven than in the challenges of this fascinating earth with its rapidly growing population with insistent demands for food.

For the past 40 years, in the United States and as a con-

sultant to the UN Food and Agriculture Organization, UNESCO, and various governments, my chief interest and work has been to "read the records" as written in the lands of some 39 countries by farmers, nations, and civilizations, and to demonstrate measures of soil and water conservation. These records clearly tell whether tillers of the soil wisely used or misused, cared for or neglected, conserved or wasted the lands which fed their people through the years. Nations rise and fall, and their rise and fall can usually be interpreted, directly or indirectly, in terms of their treatment of the land and the peasant who tilled the fields. If the farmer does not have a square deal, he will not give his lands a square deal. When the farmer is sick and apathetic and the fertility of the soil goes down, a nation declines and becomes a prey to aggressive neighbors.

Today, soils are eroding, productivity is diminishing in most of the world's cultivated and grazed lands. My findings have been that, with few exceptions, wherever mankind has lived longest in organized societies, there the lands are in worst condition.

In this world where the UN reports that more than 60 per cent of the peoples—our neighbors—are underfed, scantily clothed, and poorly housed, demographers predict a population explosion whose repercussions are already beginning to be felt. By 1970, the world population will have increased to 3.4 billion and will reach around 6 billion by the end of the century. These subsistence agrarian economies wherein the peasant farmer uses hand labor, primitive tools, and traditional methods cannot increase production to keep pace with this increase in population.

My studies lead me to the conclusion that *"civilization is running a race with famine and the outcome is still in doubt."* This doubt is not due so much to limitations of natural resources of the earth, plundered and damaged as they are,

as to the lag in the take-up of modern improved agriculture among the two-thirds of mankind who are subsistence farmers. This presents a terrifying challenge. I have seen in China, during famines, how the frail structure of civilization falls apart. People will sell their liberty, their all, for food. A starving farmer will eat his seed grain. Parents will sell their children. Starving people will follow any demagogue who promises them food. Hungry people will not keep the peace, neither will they keep their treaties, nor will they stay within their own boundaries. There is no substitute for food.

From where is this food to come? The best lands of the earth are now under cultivation. Costs of reclaiming marginal and new lands for cultivation will be higher and higher, and at best will bring into production only 8 to 11 per cent increase in area. The greatest potential increase of food stuffs, fibers, and fats for the needs of mankind's rapidly increasing numbers will come from improved production on lands already under cultivation by means of modern scientific methods. We have seen in England, Japan, the United States, and Israel, and on pilot plots in other lands, how production can be doubled or better by modern conservation farming in its various advancements. With this knowledge, we must take a new look at the teeming masses of mankind that gain only a meager living out of tilling the soil and herding their flocks. We must do this whether we like it or not—in our own interests as well as theirs.

The solution to the problems of the peasant farmer does not consist in charity gifts to hundreds of millions of poor peasants, or in lavish expenditure of money and wealth by American taxpayers. The problem is not solved until the peasant himself learns to produce more to increase his purchasing power, along with increase in facilities for exchange of his surpluses. In the last analysis, only

the peasant can save himself. We cannot compel or force him to change his ways. We can collaborate with him and win his confidence and, as a good neighbor, patiently lead him forward a step at a time to understand and use modern measures. We cannot expect the peasant farmer to make one great leap across the centuries from primitive subsistence farming into modern agriculture which is the culmination of centuries of research and work. He needs at least a generation. Unless he gets it in that time, we are lost.

In our good neighbor dealings with peasant farmers, we must gain their confidence and respect whenever we seek to render technical and other assistance, for they will not try something new until they see results for themselves. They are little moved by exhortation but usually, in time, respond to demonstrations.

It has been my practice in working with peasant farmers to identify myself with them and their problems. For example, when serving as a consultant to the British Colonial Office in West Africa, I wanted to see for myself the practice of "shifting cultivation" in the tropics. In the bush of Sierra Leone, my missionary interpreter and I stopped to talk to a Negro peasant who had cut down a patch of "bush" and, at the end of the dry season, had burned the fallen trees for the ash as a dressing of fertilizer. He had sowed seeds of upland rice in the ashes. We found him using a little short handled hoe to cover the seeds. He was very much annoyed with us and obviously wanted us to leave him alone at his work.

I smiled and took his little hoe and began to work, covering up seed grain and pulling weeds as he had done. At first he laughed at me, for I was more awkward than he. But as I kept on, he became serious, and later when I returned his hoe, he willingly answered my questions as we sat down together on the hillside and discussed problems of farmers in

other lands, of which he knew nothing. But when interpreted in terms of his own problems, he was interested.

I have used this way of identifying myself with the peasant farmer in many countries: by taking over the plowing with oxen on steep stony hillsides, using the wooden plow of the Syrian farmer—not easy I assure you—or winnowing grain with farmers in China, Yugoslavia, and elsewhere; or using the small sickle of the Bedouin nomad in Sinai and cutting the meager harvest a handful at a time. In general, I show up not quite as skillful as the peasant in his work, and this gives him a sense of superiority as he shows me how he does it. After this, I have always found him willing to talk and answer questions or try what I have to demonstrate.

The first step I take in working out a program of improved land use with conservation of soils and waters is to evaluate farmer practices in the region. This traditional agriculture has come down to the peasant through sayings, proverbs, and customs based upon a long period of trial and error. To ignore or ridicule these traditional practices is fatal to winning the confidence of the peasant in you or in your proposals. To recognize his achievements and honor him for what he has done and then to build on this foundation is my first step in proposals for demonstrations or programs of policy and works.

Especially was this true in China before the Communist take-over. We had found here and there isolated solutions to problems in the use of land and water, already worked out in whole or in part by individual farmers. Neither the farmer nor his neighbors usually appreciated the significance of his discovery. We gave recognition and honored farmers for what they had done and then engineered these primitive solutions with advanced techniques and applied them systematically in demonstration areas which the Government helped us to rent from farmers. Also, we employed the

farmer peasants to assist in carrying out the measures and simple works. In this way, we overcame one of the most difficult barriers and resistance to introduction of modern agriculture for greater production and for sustaining it with measures of soil and water conservation. When a peasant sees that these are his own practices, improved by ways he himself has helped to apply, barriers are broken down.

When the Chinese farmer saw for himself that other ways were better, he voluntarily changed his ways. While we were putting in demonstration projects in soil conservation, farming, and crop improvements, local farmers came by the hundreds to watch. Our demonstration included scientific engineering of some measures the Chinese had developed by trial and error and constructing of a system of bench terracing of slopes to conserve the rain where it fell, using only implements that local farmers had at hand. Crop yields from the demonstration project were double those prevailing previously from the same area. Thereupon, 90 per cent of the farmers of the project area called on us to help them put in the same measures on their own lands. The last I heard, the project was still continuing under the new regime. But how the individualistic Chinese farmers will survive the present rigorous program of forcing farmers into communes under strict dictatorship is hard to tell.

Eyes of the world are now on the nearly empty continent of Africa with its fabulous possibilities, occupied by only 200 million people mostly in a stage of subsistence agriculture. The native peoples still practice an Early Iron Age agriculture with primitive methods and tools which cannot possibly increase production to feed the rapidly increasing populations which are doubling their numbers in 25 to 35 years.

But the African cannot suddenly leap from such a primitive agriculture into modern conservation farming, even if

we were to supply every farmer with money and tractors. We must recognize the peculiar problems of Africa. Farming in black Africa is not the simple process as previously described, for every operation in farming the soil is related to taboos, superstitious customs, witch doctors, or juju. Witchcraft dominates all farmer practices. African chiefs, with few exceptions, are powerful reactionary forces. They have vast powers in land tenure and in allotment of parcels of land. They can crush or punish farmers who resist them. For one man to forge ahead of his fellows or his chief in new ways and successful farming is witchery and punishable. Missionaries tell of students who did excellent modern farming in school demonstrations but do traditional farming on their own lands for fear of punishment or death. For just this has frequently happened to progressive Negro farmers.

The native African takes no responsibility for land improvement, for under the usual two-year allotment system of tribal land the peasant never receives the same fields again, neither do his children inherit them. The native African male has always been a hunter and warrior. He does not take to farming easily. It has always been his wife with her little hoe who grew the food.

African lethargy, indifference, obstruction, passive resistance, and sometimes outright hostility, combined with the "heavy hand of the past," witchcraft and juju, is a terrific handicap and frustration to agricultural extension officers and demonstrators working earnestly to help the African farmer grow more food on his deteriorating lands. The crushing of individual initiative by chiefs and witchcraft stifles progress, wasting one of the greatest national assets—the initiative of peoples.

These are some of the difficulties in the way of an effective good neighbor attempt to help the African farmer win his race with famine. We cannot thrust on him what we have

learned for ourselves over generations of slow progress. He
can only take what he can use or is capable of absorbing.
It will take patient work, identifying oneself with the black
man and his problems, working with him in demonstrations,
building on his farm practices in the way the late Emory
Alvord did so successfully in Southern Rhodesia. The great
question in this race with famine is, How a sufficient number
of such dedicated men can be found in time for all sections
of Africa to save deterioration of lands and the African from
starvation? A Negro minister, after hearing me tell of what
was happening to the lands of West Africa, arose and said,
"Now we understand why hunger already done catch us."

The *fellah* or *fellaheen* of the Arab Middle East and Egypt
could well be called the "exploited farmer." From time im-
memorial the control of the ruling classes has rested on ruth-
less exploitation of the peasant. Although these peasants
have fine qualities of hardihood and pride, centuries of
exploitation and their own superstition and ignorance have
kept them from realizing the full possibilities of their lands
and themselves. There must be social justice and a more
equitable distribution of land and wealth, with opportunity
for the peasant to earn purchasing power to give him some
of the good things of life for which he is now longing. He
needs help. At best it will be a slow process, but as is evi-
dent in Israel, when the Arab fellaheen is brought face to
face with farmers who use scientific techniques and live in
a just social order of equal advantages for all the population,
they rapidly respond. It is here that Israel is a pilot area for
the Middle East in showing how old, long misused lands
can be made to produce food for increasing populations.
Where the Arab farmer has had scientific help, loans, high
wages, and guaranteed fair prices for his produce, he has
rapidly become the most prosperous farmer of Arab lands.

If we are to understand the problems of our neighbors

we must include one of the greatest burdens on farming operations around the world, including modern nations of Europe—the *fragmentation of fields*. This means land holdings have been divided into smaller and smaller parcels, separated by varying distances that cause loss in time and efficiency of the farmer. This fragmentation may have come about by inheritance, by allotments by heads of villages or tribes, or in other ways. Land so divided decreases farmer efficiency and makes it difficult to install soil and water conservation measures and to use farm machinery. Fragmentation of land is a millstone about the necks of farmers of small holdings. In some European countries fragmentation of land has become so advanced that laws have been passed to induce and help farmers to exchange land in scattered parcels and to consolidate holdings in more workable blocks. In India cooperation in the use of land is sought as means of overcoming disadvantages in fragmentation of land. Consolidation of fragmented small holdings into workable units is a goal for all lands suffering this great burden on farmers in subsistence economies.

Our good neighborliness will be effective as the peasant is trained and permitted to benefit from his own industry and thrift. Not until the peasant, growing only what he and his family need, becomes a farmer growing surpluses beyond his own needs and releasing more and more of his fellows for other labor in society, will he take his place as a prosperous farmer.

Such is the task in our time—to release the energies of more than two-thirds of mankind in their own interests, and in ours as well.

THE
SUBJUGATED

By MICHAEL SCOTT

Those everywhere, but especially in
Africa, whose freedoms have been
curtailed, who are subjugated and
downtrodden by more powerful
forces, are "neighbors" to Michael
Scott.

MICHAEL SCOTT has spent most of his years living among the poor and downtrodden in England, in India, and mainly in Africa, trying to make life more livable for them. He first went to South Africa when he was nineteen years old and worked at a rehabilitation center for Africans who had had leprosy. He took his theological training both in South Africa and in England. He was ordained an Anglican priest in 1930, and served for a short period in a fashionable West End London parish, then in a very unfashionable East End parish, until 1935 when he went out to India.

At the beginning of World War II, Mr. Scott left his parish in India to join the RAF as an airman. On being invalided out in 1943, he returned to South Africa as a curate at St. Alban's Coloured Mission in Johannesburg. Unpopular with the Government because of his loyalty to the cause of the natives, he was arrested twice and, at one point, spent three months in jail for joining them in passive resistance to a segregation law.

In 1947 Mr. Scott was asked by the Herero and other tribes of South West Africa to be their spokesman at the UN against incorporation of the Mandated Territory by the Union of South Africa. In 1949 he was granted a hearing on their behalf by the UN Trusteeship Committee. Except for one visit to report to these tribes, he has been pleading their case in Britain and at the UN ever since, coming to the US frequently on a restricted visa and living in hope of receiving an ordinary visa. He has been heard by the Trusteeship Council on three occasions, and the Assembly has resolved in his favor.

Because of his activities on behalf of the Hereros, Mr. Scott is not permitted to return to South Africa. He lives in London and is honorary director of the Africa Bureau, a group concerned for the cause of African colonial peoples which has recently proposed that a conference be held to consider the adequacy of present and projected plans of technical and financial aid to Africa.

Mr. Scott is author of *A Time to Speak.*

The Subjugated

*M*Y INTEREST in the problems of Africa dates
from the age of nineteen when I left England for Cape Town
in search of fresh air and sunshine. I had been brought up
in one of the worst slums in England where my father had
a parish on the banks of the River Itchen. It comprised the
shipbuilding yards and the area housing the people who
work in them, an area of half a square mile containing a
population of 10,000 which was listed as the second worst
slum in England. I was, however, one of the fortunate ones
favored by the circumstances of my parents which enabled
me to escape to Africa and survive the attacks of the many
diseases which were rampant in that place.

I went to a mission station called St. Raphael Faure which
was really a settlement designed for the rehabilitation of
lepers who had been cured by the then new process of
treating leprosy. Many of these cured lepers had lost some
of their limbs, some had been affected mentally, or in their
hearing or eyesight. They were for the most part Africans

and Coloured people; hence my first contact with Africa and its problems was to be confronted with the double barrier to human happiness and well-being, namely, the natural barriers of disease and death and the artificial man-made barriers of the color bar, prejudice, and actual legislation designed to preserve white supremacy or *baaskop* and to keep the African people down, and out of our civilization. For this is what so many of the laws and social customs of South Africa imply. I did not see it then as a great threat to what we have now come to call the West, but I do see it so now. South Africa is in a way a microcosm of the problems of the world in which the great contemporary battle of ideas must be thought out, and may be fought out; but we hope the fighting will be by means of non-violent weapons—weapons of peace that can preserve to the protagonists at least some semblance of a civilized existence.

It may be in the great struggles that lie ahead in Africa that some of the immortal values of tolerance and appreciation of the great variety, and intended differences, of creation will be kept, but equally there is the possibility of a repetition of Christ's crucifixion in Africa. Christianity has not always been the religion of tolerance and understanding; on the contrary, it has often been made an incentive for oppression, persecution, race discrimination—all the things that Christ would have abhorred had he known them in the form which they are practiced in this year of grace which we denote as Anno Domini 1960.

We stand at the beginning of a new period in the world's history. Perhaps it will be a period of progress and prosperity for the human race, but equally it may be a return to the Dark Ages in which hatred, violence, and intolerance will reign supreme. The fate of humanity hangs in the balance during the fateful months and years that lie ahead, and the great decision has to be made once and for all whether the

undreamed-of power that human intelligence has brought within its grasp is to be used to destroy man's attempts to build a civilization, or is to be used to construct a new order in Africa and the so-called underdeveloped countries of the world which will enable people to do more than exist—to co-operate, to understand the reasons why men are moved in the direction of conflict and the temptation to destroy what they cannot understand or what seems to threaten their security.

The age when free rein can be given to these passions, to the politicians who think they can use superior force as the sanction for their policies, is past. The new age which is dawning requires a rare combination of crusading zeal with forbearance, patience, and a willingness to use infinite pains to find the right procedures, the peaceful procedures, which can bring justice and social peace in place of the wrath and hatred which have inspired the sans-culotte of previous successful revolutions.

As humanity enters the space age armed with nuclear power, it clings for security to ideas and ideals that belong to an age that is past. And those outworn ideas and moral standards so far from bringing us any security have themselves become a menace not only to order and progress but possibly to the very existence of a civilization on this planet.

We are multiplying nationalisms which all too often end in tyranny after the first fight for freedom has been won, while we have not yet found that universal and cohesive revolutionary force which can both challenge oppression and injustice and at the same time establish law and rational discussion as a civilized method of settling the great controversies of our time. These controversies remain, however much we desire peace and confer about good will. The question is how are we going to set about analyzing them objectively and trying to solve them, whether by discussion and

negotiation, using as sanction in the last resort the threat of force, or whether we can find another method of resistance and persuasion which will not destroy all that man has attempted to achieve.

It has become a question of the survival of the human race what the beliefs of this hitherto earth-bound species are and what actions they inspire in face of this challenge. For man can now propel his engines, his missiles, and very soon himself through space at thousands of miles an hour, through outer space, and into orbit round the sun. He can communicate his ideas to the ends of the earth in no time at all. But his inventive genius, capable as it is of discovering and harnessing to human purpose some of the innermost secrets of the universe, is yet unable to bring his motives and ideas into any sort of rational conformity to his new situation on this planet and in this universe.

At a moment of history when humanity desperately needs a universal faith, religious bigotry and mythical beliefs divide mankind into a number of competing universal faiths, each one itself divided into innumerable different sects and denominations whose rivalries are almost as bitter as any that proceed from differences of race or nation.

Similarly, nationalism is an increasingly potent force in a world which desperately needs some supra-national and cohesive force if humanity is to find a way of settling its powerful differences of ideology and vital interests by civilized methods which will not result in total annihilation by nuclear weapons or, even worse, the genesis of a race of monsters on this planet through the effects of radiation.

This is the general situation in the life of man today against which the problems of race and nation which have come down to us from previous generations must be thought out if they are not to be fought out.

Against this background too must be set down some of the

facts which we have to face and which are being neglected by our statesmen in their preoccupation with power politics and advancing the day-to-day interests of their own nation or group of states. For example, Professor Waddington has estimated that by 1960 the world will have spent the equivalent of 1,000 dollars per head of the population of the world on armaments which all claim will act as a deterrent against war. The average income per head of the population of the world is less than 100 dollars per year. We may hope and pray that the deterrent may remain balanced, but it will be folly to minimize the danger of being overtaken in the rear by the ever-growing problems of population increase and underproduction and distribution of food. The yearly increase of population is about 47 million—that is to say, the equivalent of the populations of London, New York, Paris, Tokyo, and Calcutta. Two-thirds of the world's population is already imprisoned by hunger, disease, ignorance, and man-made oppression. Three out of four of them have less than $1.40 a week to spend. As D. K. Faris has pointed out, a line of hungry and suffering human beings could start at your front door and reach round the world (25 thousand miles) and return to your front door not once or twice or five times but twenty-five times. From 1937 to 1957 the line increased by two-thirds—a new circle every two years. If you drove by them in a car for ten hours every day at 50 miles per hour, it would take three and one-half years to pass by them all and the line lengthens by 20 miles every day. By the end of this century the population of the world will have more than doubled—that is to say, within the lifetime of our present teenagers. So it is very much the concern of our teenagers today if they are to inherit a world fit to live in.

Of course, some cynics will say the atom bomb will take care of that. But, of course, it will not. The atom bomb can

destroy 3 million people at one shot, but it cannot create anything. It can destroy the great industrial centers and installations, dams and communications, which alone make possible a civilization capable, in the modern sense, of sustaining life on this planet.

We stand urgently in need, therefore, of a revolutionary movement whose means will be compatible with the ends it serves and which will recall our statesmen to the basic tasks of civilization: the feeding of the hungry, healing of the sick, clothing the naked, and housing the homeless and refugees.

People, when they are hungry and ignorant and deprived of the advantages of education and the security of a civilized existence, tend to become inspired more by fanaticism and despair or hatred than by reason.

Nor must we ever forget that it was a nation which had contributed more to the civilization of Europe than perhaps any other in recent times through its science, its art and philosophy, its theology and literature, and its music that was yet driven mad by a myth of its own racial superiority. Its youth was carried away as by some demoniac Pied Piper of Hamelin and that nation was made capable, by all the modern means of communication, of committing the worst crimes against humanity that have ever been committed by any race of men. Six millions of old men, women, and children tortured deliberately, starved, and brutally done to death in the concentration camps and gas ovens of Nazi Germany.

That happened to a great and proud European nation and it can happen again. Today we try to forget that it happened because it all seems such a ghastly nightmare, but it did happen and unless mankind and its leaders can be brought to its senses to face the vast problems of our time before it gets too late, it will happen again. At present we

are being led by men in declining years who belong to an age that is gone by, whose ideas are leading them to the threat of disaster. But creeping up behind us are all the questions they have neglected to ask, let alone to answer, and it is by them that we may be engulfed unless we can reverse the process which drives humanity towards the nemesis of its own inventive genius bereft of a sense of values and conceptions of meaning and purpose in life.

As Koestler has expressed it in *The Sleepwalkers:*

Thus within the foreseeable future man will either destroy himself or take off for the stars. It is doubtful whether reasoned argument will play any significant part in the ultimate decision, but if it does a clearer insight into the evolution of ideas which led to the present predicament may be of some value. The muddle of inspiration and delusion, of visionary insight and dogmatic blindness, of millennial obsessions and disciplined double-think, may serve as a cautionary tale against the hubris of science. Our hypnotic enslavement to the numerical aspects of reality has dulled our perception of non-quantitative moral values. The resultant end-justifies-the-means ethics may be a major factor in our undoing. Conversely the example of Plato's obsession with perfect spheres, of Aristotle's arrow propelled by the surrounding air . . . Galileo's confidence tricks and Descarte's pituitary soul may have some sobering effect on the worshippers of the new Baal, lording it over the moral vacuum with his electronic brain.

Neither can we forget that it was those countries which have been amongst those longest under Christian influence that invented and constructed the atomic bomb and dropped it deliberately not as a demonstration in the sea or on a military installation or even the seat of a government but on the center of a defenseless city, killing at Hiroshimo 60 thousand civilians in one act. In *Brighter Than a Thousand Suns* we read how at the moment of impact when some of the senior scientists were watching their instruments to observe the effects, they heard some of the junior scientists in

the laboratories and passageways triumphantly imitating the
Red Indians' war cry.

Nor can we forget that racial discrimination where it has
been most rigidly enforced as a highly organized and legal-
ized system, as is apartheid in South Africa, has claimed
the sanction of a "Christian nationalism." And it has
been noticeable over the twelve years of the existence
of the United Nations, during which the question has
continued to be debated, that it is the Christian nations which side with South Africa and abstain from
voting on the grounds that the treatment of Africans
and Asians is a "purely domestic matter" for the Union
Government. Discussion of the matter according to their
interpretation of the UN Charter is tantamount to "intervention," despite interpretation given by two-thirds majori-
ties every year that discussion is necessary in any attempt to
reach peaceful solutions of a situation that member states
have adjudged to constitute a threat to peace and security.
Britain, France, Belgium, Italy, Holland, Spain, Portugal,
Sweden, Finland, Australia, New Zealand, and Canada are
the states which normally abstain in the vote on apartheid.
It is significant that those who oppose it are for the most
part the African and Asian states, the South American re-
publics, and the Muslim countries, supported by the Communist states.*

Yet there seems little hope of any peaceful solution of that
great human and moral problem without some inspired and
beneficent influence from the Christian and civilized nations
which have some bonds of kinship and culture with South
Africa. Postponement of any real attempt (as opposed to
mere repeated denunciation) to face and solve this problem
vital to the future of all Africa can only lead to an eventual

---

* In a vote of 67 to 3 (7 abstentions) in November, 1959, the dissenting
votes were cast by France, Great Britain and Portugal, all of which have
African colonies. Also see p. 7, n. (Ed.)

holocaust and terrible day of reckoning for the white race. But equally important is it to see this question against the whole background of world history and of the need to construct workable constitutions which will enable peoples of different races to cooperate together and build up a system that will work, that will enable them to produce the necessities of life and progress and appreciation of the great contribution the different races have to make to a more varied and more abundant life.

If some such constitution cannot be worked out for the vast areas of Africa inhabited by different races, inevitably racial competition and conflict will increase as they are increasing in Central Africa and show signs of spreading further into East Africa. The problem is a complex one, having important economic aspects as well as political, religious, and philosophical ones. None of them can be isolated and discussed as though the question were solely one of morality or religion or politics or economics. It is essentially a whole human problem, and any tendency to oversimplify it can only lead to inadequate or positively wrong remedies being sought.

South Africa represents a challenge to the white race to find some modus vivendi with the overwhelming majority of that country and that continent on whom depends the full utilization of its great resources. Artificial color barriers to education and to the training and use of African skills can only limit production and charge political and social life with increasing suspicion and hatred.

In South Africa, which is the most technologically advanced state in Africa with vast mineral and industrial resources, there has become entrenched a whole state system based upon the conception of race supremacy or *baaskop* to use the Afrikaanse word. By this system the white minority of two and one-half million hold absolute political

power over the rest of the population numbering ten million Africans, one million people of mixed race, and half a million people of Asian origin. The Africans, who constitute three quarters of the population, are represented by three members of Parliament in a House of Assembly of 160 members. And those three members must be white because no African may sit in Parliament or in any provincial assembly or municipal council in South Africa. This has meant that over the years the African people have been reduced to ownership of less than 13 per cent of the land. Their reservations have become grossly overpopulated and overstocked, and this has given rise to soil erosion and further reduction of the land available for their use. Thus the reserves are nothing more than reservoirs of cheap labor to supply the white man's mines, industries, farms, and domestic needs. The mines have always refused to pay Africans anything approaching normal living wages, arguing that the Africans possess land which they can use to support their wives and families in the reserves. Hence an economic system has grown up with deeply rooted vested interests on the part of heavy industry in keeping African labor cheap and keeping it migratory.

Africans have no constitutional means of redress or reform. They are not able by the normal political activities common in a democracy to secure any alleviation of the burdens and restrictions which bear so heavily on them and their movements and their choice of occupation. Pass laws similar to those which controlled the lives and movements of the English peasantry in the reigns of Edward III and Richard II, are now being extended to African women, and for the first time recently demonstrations of African women assembling to march on Pretoria were dispersed by jet fighters. The Group Areas Act, which aims at the maximum possible segregation, will involve the forcible eviction of whole popu-

lations, such as the Indians in Durban, from areas where for generations they have been accustomed to own and occupy property and engage in trade with people of all races. The aim is to remap South Africa and enforce by law the division of the country into separate socio-economic systems for each race, despite the hard economic fact that a modern industrial system tends towards integration, towards drawing people together rather than keeping them apart. And this process has been continuing apace during the whole period that apartheid has been the official policy of the Government.

Hence the time has come for a great deal of new thinking to be done about South Africa in particular and about Central and East Africa where the doctrine and practice are not yet so rigid. There are great dangers in pursuing a policy of drift, yet the British Government has declined to define its end aims in countries such as Kenya and Nyasaland and has certainly not begun to prepare the white race for the shock of finding themselves living in anything like a democracy in Africa.

The violent revolt against the white man's justice and religious beliefs in Kenya is not the only manifestation of Africans' discontent and determination to be free of all the artificial restrictions against their progress. The more civilized methods of non-cooperation and civil disobedience have been restored to on a mass scale in South Africa. Ten thousand people there served voluntary terms of imprisonment in protest against unjust laws. The barbaric Public Safety Act, threatening passive resisters with 5 years imprisonment, 500 pounds fine and/or 15 lashes, may have brought that movement to a halt for the time being. But other forms of non-cooperation have proved possible, including the boycott of transport services and "go slow" actions in mines and factories.

These non-cooperation and civil disobedience movements do not violate the principle of respect for one's opponents and take account of the necessity to recognize their intelligence and integrity. As a method, it thus seems preferable to the use of violence. But the ruling race in Africa has shown a singular lack of appreciation hitherto of Africans' efforts to conduct a civilized struggle for their own emancipation. But it may be that world events will soon begin to influence them to recognize the need for a new approach to their problems and a new relationship with the Africans on whom the future development of that continent's vast resources will depend.

Experience in South Africa has convinced me that the new revolutionary period in human history which is beginning needs the inspiration of religion and reason, as opposed to the destructive dogmas of the economic motive, group self-interest, and hatred whether based on the conception of class or nation or even social righteousness. Our struggle is the struggle of all humanity against oppression in all its forms under which when one class, or nation, or race suffers, all suffer—not least the oppressor group.

When in South Africa I joined the so-called "non-Europeans" in a civil disobedience movement against a whole state system of race discrimination, it was in the conviction that we of the white race in South Africa were suffering as grievous moral and intellectual damage through the oppression we were imposing on others as the physical damage and unhappiness it caused to those whom we oppressed. It must be remembered that South Africa is not merely a country of violent racial prejudices but a country in which the theory of race has been elevated almost into a religion and is enforced by means of a whole network of legislation designed to keep the so-called "non-European" races not only separate but inferior and to perpetuate the system of race rule known

as *baaskop*. The need in South Africa, as in the world at large, is to discover the methods and means of resistance to injustice and state tyranny which will preserve the respect which one human group should have for another while retaining its own integrity and all the values which lie behind the conception of the "dignity and worth of the human person."

There was thus no incompatibility between civil disobedience against an unjust law and the appeal which I made to the United Nations and the International Court of Justice on behalf of the Herero tribe and other oppressed people in South West Africa against their incorporation by the Union of South Africa.

On the contrary, the logic of the trend of our present period of history is against the use of force and violence to achieve any of the ends of human existence and civilization. It is a trend toward the discovery of new means and methods of resistance to abuses of state power; toward the elevation of human conscience and values; and toward the extension of the rule of international law. The system of justice must be independent of party or religious creed. There is no contradiction here. Those who deliberately choose to disobey a particular law, preferring to suffer the penalties of disobedience to being party to its imposition on others, do so from respect for the law, not disrespect, and because in principle they regard law and order as the instruments of justice and peace in the world.

Such was Christ's way. He did not disrespect Roman law, which was the highest form of law and order the world had known up to that time. But he set himself against the evils, the social and political corruption, of his time and nation even to the point of opposition to the law and the state. He was in fact convicted of treason and blasphemy, but his form of resistance issued in the highest form of expression

known to the spirit of man, namely, in the forgiveness of his enemies even during his last extremity of torture and execution. He could even find excuses for his tormentors in the most famous of all last words: *Father, forgive them; they do not know what they are doing.*